MEASUREMENTS IN THE RHEOLOGY OF FOODSTUFFS

MEASUREMENTS IN THE RHEOLOGY OF FOODSTUFFS

J. H. PRENTICE

Formerly with the National Institute for Research in Dairying, Shinfield, Reading, UK

ELSEVIER APPLIED SCIENCE PUBLISHERS
LONDON and NEW YORK

ELSEVIER APPLIED SCIENCE PUBLISHERS LTD
Ripple Road, Barking, Essex, England

Sole Distributor in the USA and Canada
ELSEVIER SCIENCE PUBLISHING CO., INC.
52 Vanderbilt Avenue, New York, NY 10017, USA

British Library Cataloguing in Publication Data

Prentice, J. H.
Measurements in the rheology of foodstuffs.
1. Rheology
I. Title
531′.11   QC189.5

ISBN 0-85334-248-2

WITH 2 TABLES AND 45 ILLUSTRATIONS

© ELSEVIER APPLIED SCIENCE PUBLISHERS LTD 1984

Typeset in Great Britain by Keyset Composition, Colchester
Printed in Great Britain by Galliard (Printers) Ltd, Great Yarmouth

Contents

Principal Symbols Used

C   Instrumental constant
F   Shape factor
H   Distance between particles
I   Moment of inertia
K   A torsional constant
P   Pressure; probability
R   A radius
W   Load
a   Radius of a sphere; a coefficient
c   Concentration; a coefficient
f   Force; a function
k   Consistency index; rate constant
l   Length
n   Rigidity; a number
r   Radius
t   Time
x   Distance

Γ   Torque
Ω   Velocity of rotation
α   Exponent of power law; constant of proportionality
β   An exponent
γ   Strain
η   Viscosity
θ   Angle
λ   Characteristic time

ρ Density

τ Stress

φ Angle; volume fraction

ω Angular velocity

Introduction

As an introduction to a classic text on the elementary calculus, a renowned teacher once began with the quotation 'What one fool can do, another can', and proceeded to lead his pupils to explore the mysteries of a new and frightening branch of mathematics with which they suddenly found themselves confronted. His success, to which the present author can vouchsafe, depended largely upon concentrating on the simple and easier parts of the subject, leaving the pupil to explore the more abstruse regions in his own good time. Whilst the present author does not claim parity with this genius of Sylvanus P. Thompson, nor would he dare impugn the intellectual status of his readers by comparing them with that of the bemused student, it is with something of the same spirit of that great teacher that he attempts to present his small contribution to rheology.

When the author accepted the invitation to write this monograph, he was advised that it should be 'pitched at graduate level'. This little innocuous phrase, however, set in motion a whole train of thoughts. Graduate of what? is the first question to be asked. Scientists who apply their skills within any of the food industries are drawn from many different disciplines. It is the author's experience that, from among his many friends and colleagues, most have become rheologists through being food scientists, rather than the other way round. The author himself, in spite of having had the benefit of a formal education in classical physics, nevertheless was obliged to learn his rheology the hard way, by studying the behaviour of the materials he encountered in his laboratory and endeavouring to mould the laws of physics that he had previously learned so that they would describe and explain the peculiarities of the behaviour he was observing. It would seem not unreasonable to suppose that others have learned their rheology in analogous ways. It is not surprising, then, that there are different views and concepts held, quite fairly, by different rheologists.

1

Some years ago there was a movement by a number of distinguished rheologists, working with such widely different materials as metals, polymers and composite materials, to develop a 'unified theory of rheology'. This was to be a mathematical statement, using the least possible number of parameters, such that by inserting appropriate experimentally determined values for these parameters, the rheological behaviour of any material would be fully predicted. It is this author's view that the one thing that was entirely predictable was that the attempt, laudable enough in its ambitious aim, would founder. The reason for this is that the problem was being tackled from the wrong end. Its proponents were attempting to fit an abstract theory to a wide range of already observed facts. Whilst one must not deny the role of deductive logic in developing a scientific theory, and there will be enough evidence of this later, nevertheless the complete scientific method requires that one starts with simple hypotheses and known facts and builds upon these with a succession of more adventurous hypotheses. This, then, at the risk of being accused of heresy, is the author's standpoint. Starting from first principles, a picture of the rheological behaviour of any material should be explained in terms of its basic structure.

In many food products it is not possible to achieve this aim completely. The product may contain many different structural elements, which may themselves exist in a variety of sizes and shapes. Or the composition of the product may vary locally within the sample. In these cases it is often only possible to explain the behaviour qualitatively and perhaps describe it in terms of a mathematical model, which is only a description and may apply only within a limited range. It is important in these cases, and they are likely to be encountered frequently, that it should be clearly understood that these models are for the purpose of describing the behaviour only and are not to be interpreted as explanations of that behaviour.

Having made this point at some length, let us return to the graduate for whom this book is intended. Clearly he will not be the graduate in mathematical physics. It is the author's conviction that the necessary and sufficient requirements for pursuing a successful career in experimental rheology are a good grounding in 'simple' science and a well-developed critical faculty. In keeping with this maxim the presentation has been kept at a level such that it requires only that mathematical skill or understanding of physics that might be acquired in a general science course before proceeding to a specialized subject.

Notwithstanding this, the reader who has the advantage of a grasp of some of the more esoteric parts of a specialized discipline may well find that it enhances his appreciation of some aspect of a rheological problem. Let it be said that, should he feel that the treatment accorded in any of the present text is not what he would have wished, he is reminded that the work is also for the graduate of a different discipline. It is hoped that he may be stimulated to think again about his own position, and he is invited to accept the challenge implied therein to rewrite that section for his own benefit with as much rigour and sophistication as he can command.

But no one should be deterred from tackling a rheological problem by the notion that rheology is a 'difficult' science. According to Einstein, of whom more will be written later, 'science is only an extension of everyday experience'. With this in mind the author has attempted to present an objective account of his views on experimental rheology within the realm of food science in the hope that it will encourage others to ponder the meaning of their measurements.

One further word may be added concerning the scope of this monograph. The ultimate criterion of acceptability of any foodstuff is determined by the reactions of the consumer. The study of consumers' subjective assessment of the structure of the product, which is manifested by its texture, is an essential component of the complete food rheologist's craft. The reader will almost certainly be aware of a number of standard works which have been written on this branch of rheology. Accordingly, no attempt has been made to trespass in that field and texture will be mentioned only where it would have been incomplete not to refer to it. The present text, as might be expected from one whose early training was in precise physical measurement, is devoted entirely to those rheological properties of food materials which can be determined by instrumental means.

At the time when this book was first contemplated, it was felt that it would be sufficient to give only a short summary of instrumental methods and their interpretation. Since that day the author has had the opportunity to discuss his subject with a number of distinguished colleagues, on both sides of the Atlantic, and these discussions have led him to revise his view. As a result, considerably more emphasis has been placed on the principles of measurement and the kind of information to be obtained by different instrumental methods and less on detailed results. It is felt that a proper interpretation of either one's own or of another's observations is possible only when the quantities measured and the accuracy achieved are properly understood. With this end in view, instrumentation has been treated in some detail, working mainly from first principles and following Sylvanus P. Thompson's excellent precept of leaving out the more abstruse matter. For those who wish to pursue this more rigorously and in greater depth there exist a number of mathematical texts to which the reader is recommended.

In keeping with the policy just outlined, having discussed the problems associated with the measurements, a few foods have been selected for consideration in some detail. The relation between their properties and their structure has been described, the treatment accorded to each being varied according to the type of material and the measurements which can usefully be made upon it. It is hoped that the different treatments may serve as examples of the different methods of approach which may be brought to bear upon any particular problem, and that the reader may be stimulated to seek solutions to his own special problems, using the same philosophy.

From time to time specialists in the rheology of different food materials write review articles in which they present a critical and up-to-date summary of the state of the art in their particular speciality. Several of these have appeared quite recently and it would be impossible to compete with their authenticity within the space of a single book. Those who have a thirst for further facts and figures will find some suggestions at the end of this book. Also, the National College of Food Technology, now at the University of Reading, some years ago began to establish a data bank of the physical properties of food products; at the time of writing the European Community is working on a similar project for the benefit of all its member states. These data banks should provide valuable sources of rheological data for those who, for one reason or another, do not have access to original papers.

Finally, it would be unthinkable to conclude this introduction without acknowledging the stimulation which the author has enjoyed in his discussions with his many friends and colleagues in the world of rheology. It is hoped that, though they may not be named, they will recognize themselves herein and accept the author's gratitude. Perhaps it would be permissible to mention just two of the elder statesmen of rheology: the late Dr Markus Reiner, for the encouragement he gave to a young physicist in his first endeavours to unravel the mysteries of non-Newtonian flow, and Dr George Scott Blair, for frequently giving him the opportunity of sharpening his wits while debating almost every facet of rheology.

CHAPTER 1

A Few Basic Ideas

The world of elementary textbook physics divided all materials into two categories: those which when not acted upon by any external agency retained their shape, and those which took up the shape of any containing vessel. The former were solids and the latter fluids. Fluids were then further subdivided into two groups: those whose characteristic feature was that, although they were inherently shapeless, nevertheless they possessed sufficient cohesiveness between their structural elements to preserve a constant volume were liquids, and the gases were those which were able to diffuse spontaneously to occupy the volume of any container. Each of these had a well-developed logos, often developed in isolation and discussed in quite different parts of the book. The food scientist may seldom be required to concern himself with the rheological properties of materials of indeterminate volume, so the remainder of this discussion will be confined to those which possess the property of cohesiveness.

It is self-evident that most food products do not behave as perfectly when acted upon by an outside force as the elementary textbooks would have us believe do solids and liquids. Nevertheless, one or other characteristic often predominates and it is this which dictates the type of measurement which is likely to be made. It will be convenient to preserve the distinction between solid and liquid materials; the food scientist will have no difficulty in recognizing the connotation of these terms by their context, though the purist may prefer to read 'sic' after each and every such use.

It is equally self-evident that not all food materials fall conveniently into these two classes. A considerable number exhibit, at some stage, both solid and liquid characteristics according to the method of observation. One large group of these comprises the plastic materials, which look as if they are solid in that they retain their form under their own weight, but can be readily deformed on the application of an outside agency, only to retain their new shape when that agency ceases to operate.

Then there are the materials which simultaneously exhibit some characteristics of both solid and liquid—the viscoelastic materials. If one wishes to draw a precise distinction, viscoelasticity is used to refer specifically to those materials which behave as if they had a solid-type (i.e. elastic) structure, but whose deformation is modified by a viscous type of behaviour. The term 'elasticoviscous' is then used to describe those 'liquids' which show some kind of elastic behaviour, such as recoil when flow ceases. When the nicety of the distinction is not important, euphony allows that the term 'viscoelastic' cover both types of behaviour.

Before, however, discussing these ambivalent properties, it is worth while giving brief consideration to the properties of the classical solids and

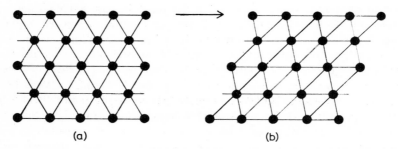

(a)   (b)

FIG. 1. Representation of a solid structure (a) at rest, (b) sheared. The arrow indicates the direction of the application of stress.

liquids. These have the simplest structure which can be envisaged. They may be considered to represent extremes, exhibiting ideal types of behaviour, between which the behaviour of all real materials will lie. First, let us look at the characteristic structure of a perfect solid. Figure 1(a), which will be familiar to most readers, may be considered to represent a block of such a solid, in which the spheres represent the structural elements making up the solid. Each structural element is acted upon by forces due to the other structural elements surrounding it and as a result the whole will be in equilibrium, with the elements a fixed distance apart. In the diagram, lines have been drawn connecting each element to its nearest neighbours. These are frequently referred to as bonds, possibly by analogy with the valency bonds of elementary chemistry. It matters little whether the structure be said to possess its peculiar characteristics because of the existence of these bonds, or through the equilibrium of the forces or because the array of elements is such that the potential energy of the system is at a minimum, as long as it is borne in mind that these three different statements are but different ways of expressing the same condition. What is important is that, just as in the zoological sciences it is important to avoid anthropomorphism, so in the present context no structural attributes should be ascribed to these bonds: they are only lines representing the components of the forces acting upon the elements, resolved in the direction of the nearest neighbours. Once this restriction is fully understood, there is no difficulty in speaking of bonds.

Let us now consider what happens when an external force is applied to this block. Suppose the force is applied tangentially to the upper plane surface in the direction indicated by the arrow in Fig. 1. The equilibrium is disturbed and the array distorted as the elements move to new equilibrium positions as in Fig. 1(b). Work is done as some of the bonds are stretched and some are compressed and this results in an increase in the potential energy stored in the system. Since the solid is supposed to be ideal, the elements are presumed to have no inertia, so that the new equilibrium positions would be taken up instantaneously. This, then, has defined one characteristic of the ideal solid—when an external force is applied, it is deformed immediately. The other characteristic, which is not so immediately obvious from the example, is that this deformation is strictly proportional to the force applied. The behaviour of a perfect solid in respect of any applied external force can therefore be expressed in terms of a single parameter, the constant of proportionality between the deformation and the force producing it, and this is known as the modulus of rigidity. The mathematical expression is simply

$$\tau = n\gamma \qquad (1)$$

A fluid is distinguished from a solid by the fact that it possesses no rigid structure. In this case the net forces between the elements are usually many orders of magnitude less than those between solid elements, and the elements themselves are in a continuous state of thermal agitation or Brownian movement. There is no static equilibrium holding the elements in a fixed array. In a gas, since there are no cohesive forces preventing it from diffusing outwards into any larger volume, the equilibrium may be thought of as labile. However, a liquid being distinguished from a gas by its cohesiveness, the net forces between the elements are attractive, though not sufficiently so to interfere with thermal agitation. By virtue of this agitation, the distribution of the elements throughout the whole is of a random nature and the equilibrium is statistical and thermodynamic. On the application of an external force there is no static equilibrium to be disturbed, the elements move to new positions and by virtue of the Brownian movement remain randomly distributed. This repositioning without modification of the structure (the thermodynamic equilibrium) will continue as long as the external force is being applied, there being no counteraction to limit it. The characteristic property in this case is that the rate at which the material deforms is proportional to the applied force, and the constant of proportionality is known as the coefficient of viscosity or, more usually, just the viscosity. Mathematically this is expressed as

$$\tau = \eta\dot{\gamma} \qquad (2)$$

The rheologist will seldom encounter such simple materials, except when they be components of his 'real' materials. The nearest he is likely to come to them is in the field of polymer science. However, polymer molecules are much too large to be treated as inertialess points. Moreover, their shape may be elongated or convoluted. Furthermore, they may have a range of both sizes and shapes, so that it may be necessary to describe these statistically by means of distribution functions. Using these ideas, theories of the rheological behaviour of polymers have been well developed. The food rheologist, however, is not likely to have much opportunity to apply these theories, except perhaps if he should be interested in single species of proteins, whose molecules are usually sufficiently like those of polymers for the same considerations to apply. For these theories the reader can do no better than consult the standard texts. The remainder of food rheologists are more likely to be concerned with materials which contain more than one constituent; maybe they will contain several.

These basic ideas have been dwelt upon at some length and at a simple level because it will be important to see later to what extent they must be modified to accommodate the presence of other constituents, how far they may apply directly to composite materials and how they can be used as 'building blocks' to describe the more complex behaviour of those systems.

Let us now carry our ideas a little further. The most general statement that can be made about the rheological behaviour of any material when it is being tested is that the deformation, or strain, is a function of the applied stress and the duration of application of that stress. As will be shown later, the properties of the sample may have been affected by what has happened to it previously, but that will not be evident as a result of a single measurement. For the moment we will ignore that possibility and consider only the properties that can be observed at the time of the measurement. The relation may be expressed simply as

$$\gamma = f(\tau, t) \tag{3}$$

Put in this form it is physically correct. The stress must be an independent variable since the laws of physics require the application of a stress to a body to produce any action and time proceeds inexorably independent of any experimenter. Nevertheless, it is not always convenient from the point of view of the instrumentation to carry out the measurement in this way, and mathematically there is no loss of generality of eqn (3) if the stress and strain are interchanged, or if either of these is replaced by a function derived from the other two.

The simplest rheological experiment that can be conceived is to apply to a sample, at zero time, a stress which, since it is applied instantaneously, shall be regarded as a step function and to observe the pattern of response. A graph showing the development of strain with time, while the stress remains constant, is known as a creep curve, a term borrowed from engineering science where many familiar materials have the property of slow elongation while under load. The creep curve for an ideal, or Hookean, solid will have the shape shown in Fig. 2(a). It shows total instantaneous response and no further flow. On the other hand, had the sample been an ideal, Newtonian, fluid, the creep curve would be a straight line through the origin with a constant slope as in Fig. 2(b). The shape of the curve distinguishes the type of material and shows up any departure from ideal behaviour. The study of this shape is the single most important way of investigating the properties of those materials which are near solid in their behaviour; it is also useful in examining very viscous fluid materials, particularly those which exhibit only very little flow within any practical times of observation. Bitumen is classically quoted as an example of this type: not many foodstuffs are likely to have the consistency of bitumen, but the method is readily applicable to a number of pastes or batters. When substantial flow occurs within the time-scale of the observations, that is, when the sample materials are more fluid, other methods of presenting the response become more convenient. In the case of an ideal liquid, if the first time derivative of the strain, i.e. the shear rate, is plotted against time when a step function of stress is applied, the curve of Fig. 2(a) again results and departure from this shape will indicate departure from Newtonian behaviour. As already suggested, it is often more convenient from the point of view of the design of the instruments and also for the interpretation of the response, that it is the motion that is imparted, as a

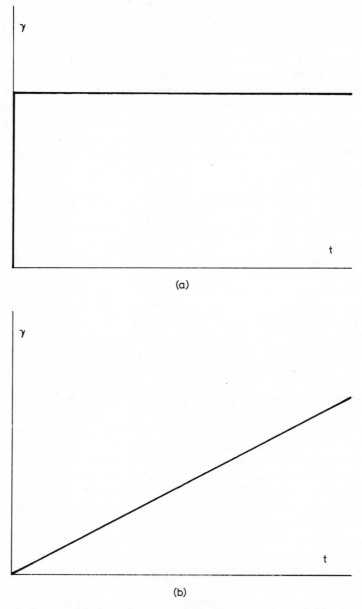

FIG. 2. Stress–strain (creep) curves: (a) Hookean solid, (b) Newtonian fluid.

step function of shear rate. The stress required to maintain that motion is then observed. If the experiment is repeated many times with different increments of shear rate, it is possible to eliminate time from the response and to obtain a curve showing the relation between the shear rate and the stress required to maintain it. For the Newtonian fluid this will be as in Fig. 2(b). Where the stress–time curves depart from the ideal of Fig. 2(a), it becomes necessary to decide upon some standard time. One popular solution is to choose infinite time and to observe the stress when the system has come to its final equilibrium. The curve relating the shear rate and the stress is the single most important curve for studying fluids and this is known as the flow curve.

When the experimenter has carried out his measurements, if he has obtained characteristic response curves similar to those described in the foregoing paragraph, it is likely that his samples are near-ideal materials. Their behaviour is completely specified by eqns (1) and (2) and they may be of little further interest to the rheologist. The rheologist comes into his own when there are significant departures from the curves of Fig. 2. It is his task to study those departures. These studies may be divided into three areas of activity. The behaviour must be described concisely, yet as completely as possible; it must be accounted for; its effect upon the subsequent use of the material should be evaluated. Simple logic would suggest that the explanation should precede the description, but rheological behaviour is often complex and the structures giving rise to it complicated, so that it is more rewarding to attempt to describe the behaviour before essaying an explanation.

It has been indicated above that rheological behaviour may be described by means of characteristic curves relating stress, strain and time and all the information may be contained therein. (It will be assumed for the present that the curves are accurate. A discussion of the limitations on accuracy and its consequences may be postponed until methods of obtaining the information have been described.) However, the presentation of information in the form of one or more curves is not necessarily the most useful form of presentation. In particular, it is not readily accessible for calculations if one wishes to use it in fulfilment of the third area of activity—the application of the data to practical problems.

It is opportune at this time to bring in the concept of rheological models. The dictionary defines a model as (a) a representation in three dimensions of a proposed structure, (b) a simplified description of a system to assist calculations and predictions. If we leave out the words 'in three dimensions', which are in fact unnecessarily limiting, since the definition could equally apply to a space of any dimensions, both definitions are apposite to rheological models. Particular attention should be paid to the choice of words in these definitions. The model is only a representation of a structure. Nowhere does it claim that it is an exact description or explanation of that structure. So, when a rheological model is used to describe a particular, observed, pattern of behaviour, care should be taken not to read too much into the details of the model. The second definition insists that the model is only a simplified description. Non-essential details have been left out in the interest of utility. The model, therefore, does not purport to replace the characteristic curves but to reduce their information content to manageable proportions.

Let us consider the architectural type of model first. If we return to our basic ideas and the definition of the behaviour of the ideal solid, the simplest mechanical device which exhibits this behaviour is a massless spring, whose extension and rigidity are related to the applied load by the equation

$$W = n\,\Delta L/L \qquad (4)$$

This is exactly analogous to eqn (1). Thus the Hookean spring may be taken as the model for an ideal solid. In an exactly similar way, the behaviour of a Newtonian fluid may be modelled by a dashpot, whose rate of extension is proportional to the applied load. It is now necessary to make the assumption that the behaviour of those materials which have properties intermediate between liquid and solid may be represented by models built up entirely by combining these two structural elements in various ways. Since the discussion is confined to materials which are assumed homogeneous and isotropic, it is sufficient to construct models in which the forces act only in one direction and which can be illustrated in the plane of the paper, without any loss of generality.

Let us now consider the flow of one of those intermediate materials and as a first step assume that it may be represented by a simple binary model, comprising one spring and one dashpot. First let us take the combination where we assume that the total stress applied to the material is shared between the spring and the dashpot, so that we may write

$$\tau_{total} = \tau_{spring} + \tau_{dashpot} \qquad (5)$$

or, from eqns (1) and (2),

$$\tau = n\gamma + \eta\dot{\gamma} \qquad (6)$$

Diagrammatically, this model is usually portrayed as in Fig. 3(a). Solving

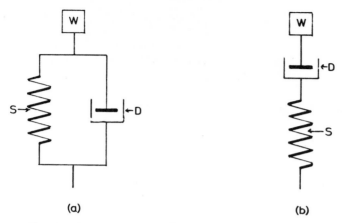

(a)　　　　　　　　　　　　　　(b)

FIG. 3. Binary models: (a) Kelvin body, (b) Maxwell body.

the differential equation (6) gives the creep curve which is

$$\gamma = \frac{\tau}{n}[1 - \exp(-n/\eta)t] \qquad (7)$$

The general shape of this curve is shown in Fig. 4(a). The material deforms most rapidly on the application of the stress, then gradually slows down and eventually reaches a constant strain asymptotically. The total deformation is limited by the rigidity of the spring, but its rate of attainment of this deformation is controlled by the damping of the dashpot. This is clearly a simple model of a 'solid' type of material. It is known as either a Kelvin body, after Lord Kelvin, who first suggested the idea of sharing the stress, or a Voigt body, since Voigt provided the mathematical expression of Kelvin's idea. By differentiating eqn (7) with respect to time, it can be seen that for short periods of time the material appears to behave as if it were fluid.

The alternative binary arrangement is for the strain to be shared between the two elements. In this case the two elements are arranged in a tandem disposition so that both take the load. This is shown diagrammatically in Fig. 3(b). The equation is now

$$\gamma_{total} = \gamma_{spring} + \gamma_{dashpot} \qquad (8)$$

or, from eqns (1) and (2),

$$\gamma = \frac{\tau}{n} + \frac{1}{\eta}\int_0^t \tau \, dt \qquad (9)$$

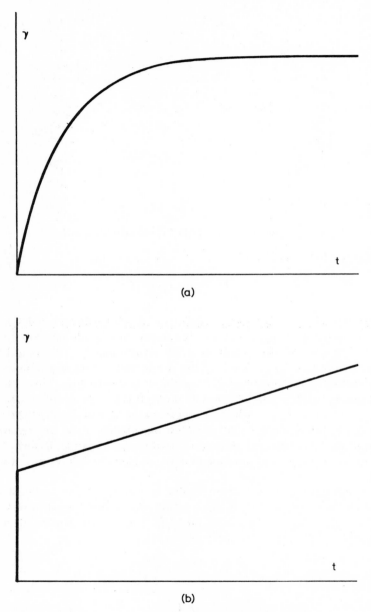

Fig. 4. Creep curves: (a) Kelvin body, (b) Maxwell body.

whence the creep curve is given by

$$\gamma = \tau\left(\frac{1}{n} + \frac{t}{\eta}\right) \tag{10}$$

and this is depicted in Fig. 4(b). The material deforms instantaneously on the application of the stress, by an amount determined by the rigidity of the spring, and then continues to creep at a constant rate. This is known as a Maxwell body. Its flow curve is indistinguishable from that of a pure liquid, but if the viscous component is very high the instantaneous response may be the dominant feature and the material will appear to resemble a solid, whilst only if the viscosity of the dashpot is low will it appear to be a liquid.

If the simple rheological experiment is carried a little further, and the stress removed, the simple Hookean spring would recover completely and immediately but the Kelvin body's recovery would be retarded, although it would eventually return to its original state. The Newtonian fluid would cease to flow once the stress had been removed, but the Maxwell body would first recover its elastic component immediately and then remain at rest.

The second part of the experiment could be carried out in a different way. Instead of removing the stress and leaving the material to recover freely, the sample could be held at the constant deformation that had been reached and the change of stress required to hold it there observed. From eqn (7) it can be shown that if the Kelvin body had reached equilibrium, the stress would remain constant, but had the equilibrium not been established, the stress would first fall immediately to that value necessary to maintain whatever strain had been reached and then would remain constant. The Maxwell body, on the other hand, would show an exponential relaxation of the stress, decaying ultimately to zero.

From the foregoing it is evident that a simple rheological experiment provides more than enough information to decide which of the two binary models is appropriate to describe the properties of the material under examination. It will be realized, and this cannot be too strongly emphasized, that these models have been derived in abstract, with no reference to the structure of real materials, using only the simplest mathematics and the one concept of a material combining both elastic and viscous properties. It is gratifying that some real materials do actually behave in a manner which bears some resemblance to these models. Unfortunately the simple models are less than adequate for many of the materials likely to be encountered by the food rheologist. The next logical step is to explore the possibility of more elaborate models. If we go back to our model of the simple solid, we recall that the structural elements were held in position by the action of forces upon them and it was tacitly assumed that on balance these forces were linear. Now we know that if these forces are London–van der Waals forces or electrostatic in origin, as for example in colloid theory, they will be far from linear. We may be tempted then to try the effect of modifying a Kelvin or a Maxwell body by making the spring non-Hookean or the dashpot non-Newtonian. Although a few rheologists have succeeded in analysing their data by means of such models, it is not a practice that can be generally recommended. It is difficult to avoid dimensional inconsistencies and it may give rise to non-analytical mathematical functions which are difficult to handle. But the most important consideration is that the virtue of a model being simple may easily be lost.

A more rewarding approach is to start with the binary units and build up further, more sophisticated models by adding springs and dashpots. There is no limit to which this process may be carried out in theory, but again the virtue of the model lies in its simplicity and its usefulness may diminish as its sophistication increases. The number of possible models increases rapidly as the number of added elements increases. There are eight possible ways in which a binary unit may be combined with one other element, and six more in which two binary elements may be combined. Not all of those combinations are useful, though. The reader may easily verify, using eqns (6) and (7), that four of the ternary and two of the quaternary arrangements degenerate into the basic binary models with only the coefficients modified. Two of the others have proved useful and their characteristics will be considered.

The model built up of a Kelvin body in tandem with a Maxwell body is the only quaternary model to have been given a specific name—the Burgers body, after the distinguished Dutch rheologist. Since the two binary modules are in tandem, the total strain is given by the simple addition of eqns (7) and (10), viz.

$$\gamma = \frac{\tau}{n_K}\left[1 - \exp\left(-\frac{n_K}{\eta_K}t\right)\right] + \tau\left(\frac{1}{n_M} + \frac{t}{\eta_M}\right) \tag{11}$$

The characteristic behaviour of this type of material is to show an instantaneous strain, followed by an exponentially decreasing creep, not decreasing to zero but to a constant linear rate of creep. On removing the stress there is an initial recovery of the original strain, followed by a further recovery of that part of the strain due to the rigidity of the Kelvin spring. The recovery is not complete as the linear component of the creep cannot be recovered. The general shape of this curve is shown in Fig. 5. If two or more Kelvin bodies are placed in tandem, the behaviour still resembles a Kelvin body in the sense that the strain is limited by the rigidities, but the attainment of the limit, the creep curve, is no longer a simple exponential, but is defined by the sum of as many exponential terms as there are Kelvin bodies in tandem. This model has some useful applications, and has been used to characterize some 'soft' solids, such as the hydrocolloid gels.

By contrast with the Burgers body, the parallel combination of a Kelvin and a Maxwell body leads to some tiresome algebra and the result is not

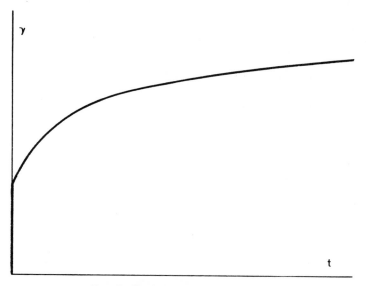

FIG. 5. Creep curve, Burgers body.

particularly helpful. Two ternary models, however, deserve mention, which may be regarded as degenerate forms of this combination. The parallel combination of a Maxwell body and a single Hookean spring is known as the standard linear solid. The name is a misnomer, as the response is anything but linear, being characterized by an instantaneous deformation followed by a creep asymptotically approaching a final finite value. If the single spring be replaced by a dashpot a model is obtained where the rate of deformation decreases exponentially with time from a higher to a lower finite value. The characteristic creep curves are depicted in Fig. 6. These models have been found useful for describing the

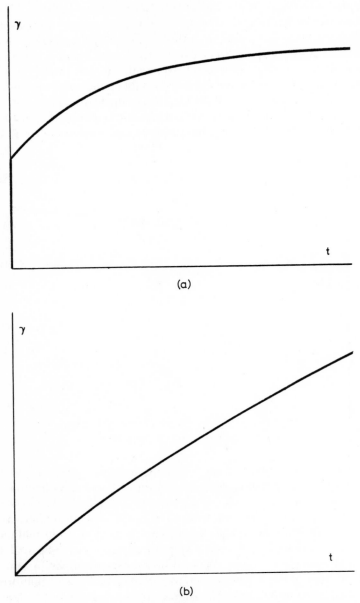

FIG. 6. Creep curves: (a) standard linear solid, (b) standard linear liquid.

behaviour of polymers just below and just above the melting point respectively, but they do not appear to have been used in the food industry.
Their relative simplicity, and the fact that only one parameter changes as
the material melts, suggests that it might be worth while exploring their
application.

From the foregoing it is seen that it is not difficult to produce equations
to describe the creep behaviour of viscoelastic materials in terms of models
composed of springs and dashpots, if the material constants are known.
Some potentially useful combinations have been described and others may
easily be derived by adding on Kelvin units in tandem as required.
Theoretically there is no limit to this process. In practice, however, there is
a limit. The experimenter is not concerned with building up model structures, but with analysing his measurements in terms of the model. There is
a practical limit to the number of constants that can be extracted from any
experimentally determined curve imposed by the precision of the determination. In general, the more complicated the model, the less useful it
becomes: it needs more parameters to describe it, these are more difficult
to evaluate from the experimental data and in the end may be less easy to
comprehend.

CHAPTER 2

Fluid Flow

In the previous chapter some simple models for viscoelastic materials were described, based only on the definitions of a Hookean solid and a Newtonian liquid and some simple algebra. These were derived in an entirely abstract manner without any reference to the properties or the structure of any real materials. We will now feed a little information into the system about the structure of some real materials and will start, this time, with the fluids.

The majority of fluids which the rheologist finds interesting contain more than one constituent. One of these is a substrate, which in its simplest form is a pure Newtonian liquid. The other, or others, may be distributed throughout the substrate as particles in suspension or large molecules in solution. The distinction between a solution and a suspension is not a clear one. Conventionally, one component is usually said to be in suspension in another when the two may be clearly seen to be so, using whatever microscopic help may be necessary, and when they may be separated using mechanical means, such as filtration, or sedimentation. The solution, on the other hand, presents a homogeneous appearance and cannot be separated mechanically. However, with the development of such aids as molecular sieves and ultrafiltration methods, the distinction is lost. For the present purposes any system will be treated as a suspension whenever the size of the particles of the disperse phase is large compared with the intermolecular distances of the substrate.

First, let us consider the effect of the concentration of the dispersed phase on the rheological properties of the suspension. A number of expressions may be found scattered about the literature which purport to explain the effect of the suspended matter. Some are purely empirical, in which case they have probably been found by their champions to apply to a particular material or group of materials with which they were at that time concerned. These need not concern us further for the moment, except to stress that they have their place when it is required to estimate the properties of a sample to which they are known to apply, by interpolating between measured values obtained at some fixed concentrations. They give no insight into the mechanism which gives rise to the properties of the material and are unlikely to have any value for predicting the properties of an unknown material. Other expressions have been advanced on theoretical grounds in which attempts have been made to evaluate the effect of any structural characteristics of the material on its rheological behaviour.

There are two points of view from which such theories may be derived. One approach is to consider the flow pattern in the continuous medium and the effects that the presence of any inclusion may have on that pattern. This will be called the hydrodynamic approach. The other is to consider the effects of any structure or pseudo-structure which might develop because of attractive or repulsive forces acting between the suspended particles. This will be called the network approach. It should be self-evident that the hydrodynamic approach is likely to be more fitting for the more fluid systems where viscosity is the main property likely to be of interest, whilst the network approach will be the more readily applicable for those materials which show pronounced elastic properties. Nevertheless, in the fairly wide grey area between the two extremes there are cases when each theory appears to explain some of the observed facts, even if not all. More generally, it is to be expected that in most materials both hydrodynamic and structural forces are at work and that one or other may be expected to predominate as the material more nearly resembles either a liquid or a solid. In view of the complexity of the structural elements which exist in the majority of ordinary food materials compared with the very simple structures which must be proposed in order to build up a manageable theory, it would be somewhat surprising if the situation were otherwise.

Let us consider the hydrodynamic approach first. The basis of this may be traced to an early paper published by Einstein, who investigated the disturbance of the flow field when a continuous medium contained a single rigid spherical inclusion which was small compared with the dimensions of the sample. His conclusion was that the apparent viscosity of the medium was increased by an amount proportional to the volume of the inclusion, namely

$$\eta' = \eta_0(1 + \alpha\varphi) \tag{12}$$

where φ is the volume of the inclusion expressed as a fraction of the total sample volume and α is a constant, whose value he put at 2·5. If the argument is extended to a dispersion containing a number of such inclusions, the same result will apply as long as each included particle is remote enough from any of its neighbours so that the regions where they cause any disturbance in the pattern of flow do not overlap. In other words, the equation may be applied directly to sufficiently dilute suspensions. Concentration is more usually expressed in terms of the weight of suspended particles per unit volume, so Einstein's formula may be rewritten

$$\eta' = \eta_0 \left(1 + \frac{\alpha c}{\rho_\alpha} \right) \tag{13}$$

where c is the concentration on this basis and ρ_α is the density of the inclusions. As long as c is small and the dispersed phase in the form of solid spheres, the formula will apply; the size of the spheres or any distribution of their sizes if they are not equal does not enter into it. However, it has been shown that if the spheres are liquid, since during flow they are in a shear field, the forces acting tangentially over their surface vary from their equator to their poles and some circulation is set up within them. The energy dissipated in this manner must also be included in the energy balance and the factor is no longer 2·5, but must be modified to take account of the viscosity of the dispersed phase. This might seem to be a serious limitation if one wishes to apply Einstein's equation to food products, since in many of them both the continuous and the dispersed phases are liquid or semi-liquid. Fortunately this is not so. In most food suspensions the dispersed material is coated with a surface-active layer, which may be a high viscosity liquid, or a viscoelastic material, or even a solid. The primary reason for incorporating such a material in the recipe is usually to stabilize the structure of the product, but in so doing it more or less effectively acts as a barrier between the continuous and the dispersed phases. As a result, any circulation within the dispersed phase is minimal and any effect it may have on the validity of Einstein's equation is also minimal.

So far only spherical inclusions have been considered. The sphere may be considered as the ultimate symmetrical shape and as such has the unique characteristic that when placed in a flow field it always presents the same geometrical configuration normal to the lines of flow and hence has the same resistance to that flow. At the other extreme we may consider an infinitely thin fibril. This will immediately align itself along the streamlines so as to present the minimum resistance and it should be self-evident that in this case the perturbation caused by its presence is limited to its own volume and the constant of proportionality in the Einstein equation becomes 1 instead of 2·5. All other shapes may be expected to lie somewhere between these two extremes. In order to allow for this, the Einstein equation must be modified by a shape factor, i.e.

$$\eta' = \eta_0 \left(1 + 2 \cdot 5 F \frac{c}{\rho_\alpha} \right) \qquad (14)$$

where F lies between 0·4 for infinitely thin fibrils and 1 for perfect spheres. Again, this is not such a serious limitation as might be feared. In many food products, the dispersed phase being liquid, the forces of surface tension act in such a way as to constrain these inclusions towards a globular shape so that they approximate to spheres.

Another aspect of the effect of shape of the suspended particles may be seen if we consider what happens when the surface of an inclusion has reentrant areas, for example, when it is shaped like a wrinkled pea. When a body of this shape rotates about its centre, the envelope of the volume swept out is more or less spherical and the body will not necessarily take up any preferred orientation in the field of flow. However, as it rotates in that field, it carries with it some of the continuous medium trapped in its reentrant regions, so that its effective volume is greater than its true displacement volume. In this case φ in the original equation must be calculated on the basis of the swept-out volume and not by dividing the concentration by the density. Then the theory still holds. An extreme example of this type of correction occurs when the dispersed phase is porous almost in the manner of a sponge. One common example of this is the casein micelle in milk. This is an agglomeration of subunits and is roughly spherical in shape, but traps a considerable amount of the aqueous serum in its interstices. The combined micelle plus entrapped serum is the unit which has to be considered as affecting the flow field. In effect, this may be said to reduce the value of the density to be used in calculating the volume fraction—in a dilute suspension the amount of serum trapped in the interstices has negligible effect on the volume of the continuous phase.

So far it has been assumed that there is no interaction other than purely mechanical between the material making up the two phases. Where these materials are mutually repellent, such as oil and water, this is probably a safe assumption. However, in many food materials the continuous phase is an aqueous solution and the dispersed phase contains material, such as proteinaceous matter, which has some affinity for water, though not dissolving in it. As a result of these forces of attraction, one or more layers of molecules of water may be 'bound' to the surface of the suspended droplet and rotate with it. In other words, the hydrodynamic surface of the sphere no longer coincides with the surface which may be observed by microscopy or other visual means, but is somewhere outside it. It is this solvated particle which is now the unit affecting the field of flow. Again the viscosity increase may appear disproportionate to the concentration, or the effective density to have been reduced. The casein micelle is again a good example of this type of behaviour. Whilst all observers do not agree on the exact magnitude of the effect, because of differences in the assumptions they have made, it would appear that the hydrodynamic diameter of the micelle in milk serum in flow is somewhere between 1·2 and 1·5 times its observable diameter.

So it can be seen that, for dilute suspensions, whilst it may be expected that there is some proportionality between the concentration of the disperse phase and the increase in viscosity of the suspension over that of the continuous medium alone, this proportionality may be modified by the shape, but not the size, of the suspended particles and by any interactions which may occur between the two phases. Nevertheless, it is a good starting point for many food materials where the effect of these two factors may be small. As yet the term 'dilute' has not been adequately defined. Strictly, Einstein's derivation can be applied only if the suspended particles are so sparsely distributed throughout the sample that the probability of any two of them coming within each other's sphere of influence when the spatial distribution of the particles is random, is vanishingly small. If, instead of using the rigorous term 'vanishingly small probability', we replace it by a more practical concept, we may say that Einstein's law applies at any concentration such that the mutual interference of the particles does not have a significant effect, taking into consideration the limits of precision of any measurement which may be made. Using this criterion, suspensions containing less than about 1% of suspended matter may usually be considered dilute, unless the particles are particularly elongated. Only when the viscometry is particularly precise would it be possible to establish a significant departure from the law. For many purposes, concentrations up to a few per cent may still be considered sufficiently dilute.

The next stage is to consider what may happen when the suspended particles are closer together, so that the probability that any particle comes near enough to another to be within its hydrodynamic influence cannot be ignored. As a first approximation we may assume that one particle has the effect predicted by Einstein, but that on the addition of a second particle this behaves as the first except that it is now in a medium whose viscosity has already been enhanced by the presence of the first. Proceeding in this way until all the suspended particles have been accounted for, we arrive at an expression, derived by Brinkman,

$$\eta' = \eta_0(1 + \varphi)^{2 \cdot 5} \qquad (15)$$

When the term in parentheses is expanded as a series, this expression becomes

$$\eta' = \eta_0[1 + 2 \cdot 5\varphi + O(\varphi^2)] \qquad (16)$$

In other words, it is the original Einstein equation with an additional correction which is important only when terms of the order of the square of the concentration become important. The general shape of the curve connecting viscosity with concentration is now roughly linear at low concentrations, but curves away upwards as the concentration increases. This is, of course, just what is observed experimentally. The Einstein equation tends to underestimate the increase of viscosity when the concentration is moderate. By comparing the two equations it can be seen that the viscosities predicted differ by less than 0·02% when the volume concentration is 1%, but this increases to about 0·5% as the concentration rises to 5% and exceeds 1% above about 7·5%. If Brinkman's analysis of the problem is correct, these figures give a measure of the limits to be set on the term 'dilute' as defined above. However, this line of reasoning still applies only to the situation where the particles are sufficiently far apart to move independently, although they may come within each other's hydro-dynamic field. Of course, the same modifications for the effects of shape and solvation still apply. As before, the upper limit of concentration for which this equation may be valid is not easily defined, but it has been shown in favourable cases that it is a fair approximation up to quite high concentrations of the order of 20% or more.

Let us now consider what happens in more concentrated suspensions. In Fig. 7 it will be seen that if particle A attempts to overtake particle B by virtue of its motion in the shear field, a collision is likely to occur. Suppose, in fact, such a collision does occur. If the suspended particles are perfectly elastic, the two colliding particles will change directions and velocity but there will be no change in their combined momentum and there will be no net gain or loss of energy in the system as a whole. So that, taken over the whole sample, perfectly elastic collisions between the suspended particles will have no effect on the observed viscosity. On the other hand, if the particles are not perfectly elastic, some of the energy due to the motion will be absorbed and will appear as heat. Since it is implicitly assumed throughout that the temperature remains constant, it must also be assumed that this heat is immediately conducted away by the thermostatting system. The net result is that more energy must be supplied to maintain the same motion. In other words, inelastic collisions between suspended particles will result in an increase in the apparent viscosity of the sample. However, the frequency of the collisions, and hence the extra stress, will evidently be proportional to the shear rate, so that the proportionality between total

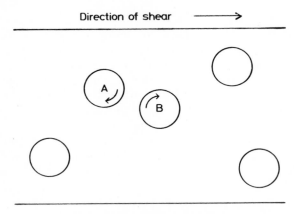

FIG. 7. Suspended particles in flow.

stress and shear rate will be retained, i.e. the suspension will still behave as a Newtonian fluid but with an enhanced viscosity.

In practice, actual collisions in the sense that physical contact is made are unlikely to occur. Because they are travelling in a shear field, the particles will have acquired a rotary motion. It is readily seen that, in the absence of any close neighbours, each particle will rotate with an angular velocity ω equal to one-half of the shear rate $\dot{\gamma}$. As two spheres approach, either by reason of one overtaking the other as in the previous example, or because of random fluctuations due to Brownian motion, the local shear rate in the medium between them would rise rapidly, since their opposing surfaces are rotating in opposite directions, as indicated by the arrows on A and B in Fig. 7. The reaction to this is to impose a couple on the pair, relative to the suspending fluid in motion, and this causes them to rotate as a dumbbell until A has overtaken B and the shearing motion causes them to separate again. Because of the rotation of these dumbbells the fluid will have a viscosity greater than that predicted had all the particles been independent.

In order to indicate the nature of this effect we may proceed as follows: Consider a suspension of uniform spheres of radius a in a continuous medium of viscosity η_s.

A shear stress τ is applied such that the suspension is flowing with a shear rate $\dot{\gamma}$.

The spheres are then rotating with angular velocity $\omega = \frac{1}{2}\dot{\gamma}$.

Let us denote the probability that a particle is free to rotate independently as P_1 and the probability that two particles rotate as a dumbbell as P_2.

Writing k_f and k_d as the specific rate constants for the formation and dissociation of doublets, the equilibrium condition may be expressed as $P_2 \underset{k_f}{\overset{k_d}{\rightleftharpoons}} 2P_1$.

On applying a shear a second mechanism is introduced for the decomposition of doublets; if this has a specific rate constant k_s, this gives rise to the reaction $P_2 \overset{k_s}{\rightarrow} 2P_1$.

Let the number of singlets and doublets per unit volume be n_1 and n_2.

Then the rate of doublet formation may be written

$$dn_2/dt = k_f n_1^2 - (k_d + k_s) n_2$$

When the steady state has been established, $dn_2/dt = 0$.

Therefore

$$\frac{n_2}{n_1} = \frac{k_f}{k_d}\left[1 + \frac{k_s}{k_d}\right]^{-1}$$

At zero shear rate $k_s = 0$ and the zero shear concentration of singlets and doublets $(n_1)_0$ and $(n_2)_0$ are related by

$$\frac{(n_1)_0^2}{(n_2)_0} = \frac{k_d}{k_f}$$

Now assume a relationship between the viscosity of the suspension and the concentration of singlets and doublets

$$\eta = \eta_s[f_1 n_1 + f_2 n_2]$$

where f_1 and f_2 are functions of n_1 and n_2 respectively but not of the shear rate $\dot{\gamma}$.

Putting n as the total number of spheres $(= n_1 + n_2)$

$$\eta = \eta_s[f_1 n + (f_2 - 2f_1)n_2]$$

At $\dot\gamma = 0$, $n_2 = (n_2)_0$ and hence

$$\frac{\eta_0}{\eta_s} = f_1 n + (f_2 - 2f_1)(n_2)_0$$

Assume that at infinite shear rate all the doublets will be dissociated,

$$\frac{\eta_\infty}{\eta_s} = f_1 n$$

This is the Einstein type of equation.
Combining the two previous equations gives

$$\frac{\eta - \eta_\infty}{\eta_0 - \eta_\infty} = \frac{n_2}{(n_2)_0}$$

and

$$\frac{n_2}{(n_2)_0} = \frac{n_1^2}{(n_1)_0^2}\left[1 + \frac{k_s}{k_d}\right]^{-1}$$

If the number of doublets is small, n_1 is not very different from $(n_1)_0$.
Therefore

$$\frac{\eta - \eta_\infty}{\eta_0 - \eta_\infty} \simeq \left[1 + \frac{k_s}{k_d}\right]^{-1}$$

As k_s and k_d are first-order rate constants, each must be related to the reciprocal of a mean lifetime.
Let t_0 be the mean lifetime of a doublet undergoing thermal decomposition and t_s the mean lifetime of a doublet undergoing dissociation by shear.
Then

$$\frac{\eta - \eta_\infty}{\eta_0 - \eta_\infty} \simeq \left[1 + \frac{t_0}{t_s}\right]^{-1}$$

t_0 is the time required for the two particles to diffuse apart a distance X such that $t_0 = X^2/2D$, where $D = kT/6\pi a\eta$.
The distance X which the particles must diffuse before they are considered as singlets again must be proportional to their radii a.
Put

$$X^2 = \alpha_0 a^2$$

We get

$$t_0 = \frac{3\alpha_0 \eta a^3}{kT}$$

The lifetime of a doublet dissociating under shear is the time taken for it to rotate from the position of formation to the position of disruption. Now the common axis of a doublet at the moment of pairing may make any angle between 0 and $-\pi/2$ with the direction of flow and in a random situation all angles are equally probable. From the symmetry of the situation relative to the shear field, it can be seen that the pair may be expected to dissociate again with their common axis at any angle between 0 and $\pi/2$ with the direction of flow, again with equal probability. We may then with perfect generality take the mean rotation of a pair as $\pi/2$.

The angular velocity of rotation of the doublet ω_2 is proportional to the shear rate ($= \alpha_1 \dot{\gamma}$, say).

Whence the mean lifetime of the dissociating doublet t_s is given by

$$t_s = \alpha_1 \frac{\pi}{2} \cdot \dot{\gamma}^{-1} = \alpha_s \dot{\gamma}^{-1}$$

Then

$$\frac{t_0}{t_s} = \frac{3\alpha_0 \eta a^3}{kT} \cdot \frac{\dot{\gamma}}{\alpha_s} = \frac{3\alpha_0 a^3}{\alpha_s kT} \cdot \tau$$

Whence

$$\frac{\eta - \eta_\infty}{\eta_0 - \eta_\infty} \simeq \left[1 + \frac{3\alpha_0 a^3}{\alpha_s kT} \cdot \tau \right]^{-1}$$

Writing

$$\tau_c = \frac{\alpha_s kT}{3\alpha_0 a^3}$$

We get

$$\frac{\eta - \eta_\infty}{\eta_0 - \eta_\infty} \simeq \left[1 + \frac{\tau}{\tau_c} \right]^{-1} \tag{17}$$

This expression shows that, by virtue of the particles being sufficiently close for 'collisions' to occur as the result of Brownian movement, the viscosity at any finite rate of shear should exceed the value given by a simple concentration dependence. The theory is obviously far from complete. For example, it does not consider the possibility of triplet or higher-order formations, which must increase as the concentration increases; it does not allow the zero shear rate viscosity to be calculated, unless one makes further assumptions about the values of f_2 and $(n_2)_0$. Clearly, $(n_2)_0$ will increase as the spheres become more closely packed, and a lower bound may be estimated for f_2 by assuming that the spheres rotate in close contact. On the other hand, it is of interest since it shows in a semi-quantitative way that any suspension of spheres may be expected to exhibit non-Newtonian behaviour as well as a viscosity in excess of the Einstein value.

Before leaving the hydrodynamic approach completely, we must consider another possibility. In the foregoing paragraphs it has been assumed that, apart from being acted upon by hydrodynamic forces, the particles possess only volume. In fact every particle is surrounded by a field of forces (gravitational, van der Waals, electrical charge) so that simple 'collisions' are unlikely. If the particles are moving together with sufficient momentum, they eventually reach a position in each other's field such that the various forces are in equilibrium and in this position the particles form a stable pair. They are then separated by a finite though small distance. (This is a situation well known to colloid scientists.) As long as it exists, the pair will rotate as a dumbbell in the flow, sweeping out as explained above a larger volume in the continuous medium than that which its constituents would sweep out individually. There are two effects of this. One is the increased stress already described which is necessary to maintain the shear rate as a result of this greater effective volume. The other is a 'knock-on' effect. By reason of sweeping out a greater volume, there is an increased chance that one or other member of this pair will encounter a third particle. In this way aggregates of several particles may form temporarily and rotate as a whole. But first, let us consider what is happening to the rotating pair. There are two distinct possibilities for what happens after the faster particle has overtaken the slower. One is that the difference in the hydrodynamic forces on the two particles in the direction of flow is sufficient to pull them apart and they continue their flow independently until they encounter further particles. The other is that the particles will continue to rotate as a pair until its axis lies along the direction of flow, in which position it presents the least resistance to that flow. Which possibility will occur will, of course, depend on the relative values of the forces acting on the particles. This, in turn, for any one system and any one rate of flow will depend on the orientation of the plane of revolution of the pair. If the rotation takes place in the same plane as that in which the direction of flow lies, the forces tending to separate the particles will be greatest. If the plane of rotation lies nearly normal to the direction of flow, the forces tending to separate the particles will be small and separation is less likely.

We must now consider the extreme situation where simple rotations become impossible. Figure 8 represents a cross-section of a suspension of

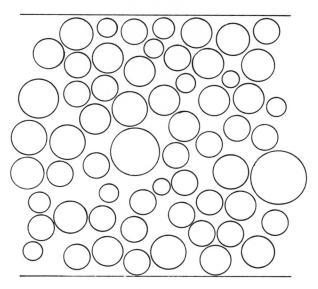

FIG. 8. Random distribution of particles suspended in a concentrated dispersion at rest.

particles having a volume concentration of 50%. The particles may be considered to be initially in equilibrium when the suspension is at rest. They are distributed in a random manner throughout the sample, subject only to the requirement that they are all discrete, i.e. each particle lies outside the net interparticle energy barrier of every other. The position of each will be only a mean position since each will be in Brownian motion, though if the particles are sufficiently large, such as, for example, the fat globules in a dairy cream, the amount of Brownian movement will be small. Suppose the suspension is now caused to be sheared. In the first instance the array will be distorted, but anything resembling flow is unlikely. Since the array is distorted away from its equilibrium state, which is, by definition, a position of minimum potential energy, some energy will have been expended in the process. So far the sample has behaved in a manner not unlike a solid. However, if the stress were now removed, the particles would rapidly resume a new equilibrium array; the individual particles would not necessarily return to exactly their original positions, but on average the array would be similar to the original. While the array was resuming its minimum potential energy condition, a stress would be exerted on the boundaries, but this would rapidly disappear. The sample would appear to have behaved as if it were viscoelastic. If, instead, the shearing were to be continued, a point would soon be reached in which pairs and other aggregates formed and these begin to rotate, though by virtue of the crowding of the particles it is evident that this rotation will be hindered and the aggregates themselves deformed in order to accomplish this rotation. This hindered rotation, in which the aggregates themselves collide and possibly make new aggregates in the process, will involve a considerable expenditure of energy. Hence, to maintain a steady rate of

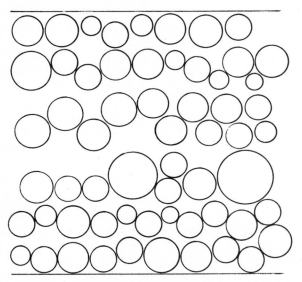

FIG. 9. Particles as in Fig. 8, but arranged in 'rafts' as a result of shear.

shear, the stress must rise steeply. Once again, if the stress be removed and the shear cease, the individual particles will not return to their original positions, but will fall back to a new random array (with minimum potential energy) in as nearly as possible the positions in which they find themselves. However, if the shear continues, remembering that pairs rotating in the plane of shear will be more likely to break up than those rotating in the plane normal to this, the eventual tendency will be for the particles to form themselves into rafts moving along the streamlines. Figure 9 shows such a situation. The greater the shear rate, the greater the tendency for these rafts to form and the less the tendency for aggregates rotating in the shear plane to exist. This condition is the one in which the resistance to flow caused by the presence of the particles is least. However, the transition from random array and aggregates to this ordered pattern can occur only if the material is continuously sheared and necessarily is far from instantaneous. During this transition the stress required to maintain a shear rate will progressively decrease, approaching its final value asymptotically. The general shape of the stress–strain curve will therefore look like that drawn in Fig. 10. If the shear ceases after the establishment of this dynamic equilibrium the particles will readily fall back into a new array

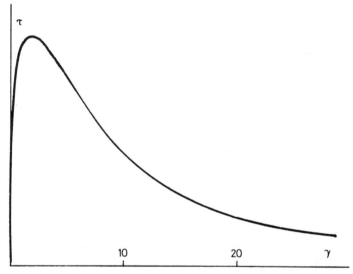

FIG. 10. 'Overshoot' phenomenon: transient response at onset of shearing.

with minimum potential energy and the stress relax quickly. So the sample which originally appeared viscoelastic now appears nearer to a true fluid, although it is true that the stress required to maintain any particular shear rate is no longer proportional to that shear rate. Rather the apparent viscosity decreases as the shear rate increases, as shown in Fig. 11. Furthermore, it will be apparent that the viscosity is no longer directly related to the concentration of the suspended particles. The controlling influence is now the 'crowding' effect and this increases very rapidly as the concentration increases. Moreover, it is no longer independent of the distribution of particle sizes. An array of spheres of uniform size can move freely in any direction when they occupy less than 52·4% of the total

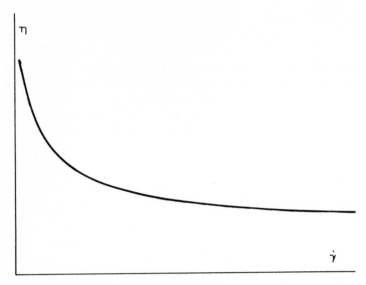

FIG. 11. Typical shear-thinning behaviour of a concentrated suspension of spheres.

volume or freely in one direction only if they occupy less than 60·5% of the volume. At any higher concentration, flow is not possible. However, when the spheres are not of equal size these restrictions are somewhat modified. The smaller spheres may move in the spaces between the larger ones and some flow is possible up to considerably higher concentrations if the size distribution is favourable. A typical example is the flow of 'plastic cream', the high fat cream which is the precursor of butter in some continuous butter-making processes. Although this contains around 80% globular fat it is nevertheless capable of plastic flow. In this case globules vary in diameter from about 10 μm down to less than 1 μm, only a small number being at the top end of the range, most of the fat being in globules of about 2–4 μm diameter.

It only remains to add the familiar rider that the shape of the suspended particles will exert an influence on the above conclusions. Whereas, when the concentration of the particles was low, an elongated particle made a lower contribution to the viscosity of the suspension than a spherical one, it should now be obvious that long particles will not only sweep out larger volumes as they rotate, but will also be much more prone to collide as they rotate and to form entanglements, so that the effect of hindered rotation will set in at a lower concentration. Anticipating what will be discussed in more detail later, we can see that in these circumstances it is quite possible for the elongated particles, being distributed randomly throughout the suspending medium, to make a tangled network (as distinct from an orderly one) at quite low concentrations of the order of a few per cent or even less. A network of this kind will naturally give rise to some form of rigidity in the sample. When the stress is first applied to this sample, some of the stress may first be used to overcome this rigidity and, by imposing some order on the network of suspended particles as they tend to become aligned along the direction of shear, may ultimately break down the structure. Here we have another non-Newtonian phenomenon, a material possessing a yield value and when the stresses exceed this yield value, it flows with a decreasing resistance to the flow as the stress increases.

To recapitulate, we have shown in the foregoing paragraphs that, by considering only the spatial relationship of discrete particles suspended in a medium, we can predict both a dependence of the viscosity on the volume fraction occupied by those particles and various non-Newtonian characteristics of behaviour which appear as the concentration increases. At low concentrations, when it is possible to make some simple plausible assumptions, these predictions may be quantitative; at higher concentrations they are no more than qualitative.

CHAPTER 3

Networks

Whilst the hydrodynamic approach outlined in the preceding chapter considers only the purely mechanical effects which arise when the particles in a suspension approach one another, the network approach considers the forces of attraction and repulsion which exist between the particles and attempts to evaluate the effect of these forces on the properties of the sample as a whole.

As before, we may start with the dilute suspension of spherical particles. If the concentration is sufficiently low and they are distributed at random throughout the suspending medium, the probability that two will be close enough to come within each other's field of force is so small that it may be discounted. So that the conditions of Einstein's equation are unaffected and we may apply it, or one of its modified forms, with confidence. As the concentration increases, the number of particles coming within the field of force of at least one other rapidly escalates, so the Einstein conditions no longer apply.

If we consider, in the first instance, a pair of particles assumed for the time being to be spheres, then if their common axis lies at an angle to the direction of flow, the net stress applied to one will be different from that applied to the other and the pair will tend to rotate in the stream about an axis normal both to their common axis and to the direction of flow. However, at the same time the thermal forces (associated with Brownian motion) will tend to restore the random distribution. The net result is a balance in which the pairs are aligned in such a way that on average the axes lie at an angle to the direction of flow, instead of being randomly distributed as when the sample was at rest. The force required to preserve the alignment shows itself as an excess over that which would be required to maintain the flow were the particles all discrete. The probability of a sphere being in any position in the sample is proportional to the concentration of the spheres in the sample. To a first approximation then, as long as the sample is sufficiently dilute, the probability of two spheres being close enough to form a pair is proportional to the square of the concentration. Therefore, without enquiring into the nature of the balance of the streaming and thermal forces, it can be seen that the viscosity increase is proportional to the square of the concentration and the equation may be written in general terms

$$\eta' = \eta_0[1 + 2 \cdot 5\varphi + c\varphi^2] \tag{18}$$

where c is an as yet undetermined factor. This differs from the equation derived by Brinkman only in that that equation includes terms of a higher order than the square of the concentration.

As the concentration increases, the probability of higher aggregates consisting of three or more particles increases rapidly. As the aggregates increase in complexity and in number a simple realignment in the direction of flow becomes less and less possible and it is necessary to consider other factors as well. One of the effects of a differential stress on the two units of a pair is that the two units will tend to become either pulled apart or forced closer together, according to whether the component of that stress difference in the direction of flow is a tension or a compression. In terms of the network theory this is usually referred to as stretching or compressing a bond. It must be remembered that this is only a convenient shorthand. The bond has no real existence; it exists only by virtue of an equilibrium of forces between the two particles. Unlike a normal physical linkage, either stretching or compressing the bond requires the expenditure of energy and this energy is released on returning to the normal equilibrium position. If the suspension is sufficiently concentrated for an appreciable network to form, the first effect of the application of a stress to the sample is for some energy to be used up in the translation of the network, i.e. in flow, but for some of the stress also to be used up within the network as it becomes distorted from its original equilibrium shape. If the stress is removed, the network recovers its original configuration, though not instantaneously as in a rigid structure, since it is necessary for the fluid of the continuous phase to flow back through the interstices as the configuration recovers. The sample is viscoelastic. If, on the other hand, the stress continues, the bonds between the particles will begin to break. Let us consider a single chain in the network in a plane parallel to the direction of the stress. In a concentrated suspension there will be many such chains oriented in all directions. The component of stress along a chain will be proportional to the cosine of the angle of inclination of the chain to the direction of the stress and to that fraction of the stress that that one chain supports. If the angle is θ and there are n such chains, the average force acting on any one chain may be written

$$f_c = \sigma \left\langle \frac{\cos \theta}{n} \right\rangle$$

If the distribution is completely random, this is equal to

$$f_c = \sigma/n\sqrt{2} \tag{19}$$

This force will break all the bonds whose strength it exceeds. The fraction of bonds which will ultimately be broken for a given stress can be determined only if the distribution of bond strengths in the direction along the chains is completely known.

However, let us return to the situation in the viscometer, where it is an increasing strain which is being applied. At first the strain corresponds to the deformation of the network and the stress builds up proportional to the elastic energy stored in the deformed network. At some point this stress becomes sufficient to cause the weakest bond to break and flow has commenced. When a bond breaks, the chain containing that bond no longer supports its share of the stress so that the stress per chain (f_c above) is increased and the likelihood of the breaking of another bond whose strength is only marginally greater is increased. It is easy to see that, as this process of breaking bonds proceeds, if the distribution of bond strengths is right, a situation will soon be reached where catastrophic breakdown of the network occurs and the stress will no longer increase with applied strain but will begin to fall, giving a curve such as Fig. 10. It will be evident from eqn (19) that the greater the number of chains, the greater the maximum stress before flow begins. Since the number of chains forming depends on the concentration of the particles in the suspension, the amount of 'overshoot' will therefore increase as the concentration increases.

When a bond is broken, the two particles originally joined by it will commence to move apart under the action of the differential force applied to the ends of the chain which includes that bond. As they move apart, the continuous medium must flow into the space formed. When the distance apart has become great enough, a nearby particle, either free, or from another chain, may begin to move into the vacated space and the chain will eventually be reformed. If we assume that the particles in breaking the bond move according to Stokes' Law and that the harmonic mean radius of the two particles is R, the time required for complete separation, or reforming, may be calculated to be

$$t = \frac{3\pi\eta_0 R^2}{\sigma\sqrt{2}} \quad \ln \quad \frac{H_1}{H_0}$$

where H_0 is the separation when bound and H_1 is the separation at which the hydrodynamic interaction becomes negligible. In practice, in a concentrated suspension, H_1 is limited by the fact that, by the time the separation is equal to a particle diameter, another particle is already moving in, so that H_1 has an upper bound of about $2R$. The shear rate, then, is related to the reciprocal of this time and may be expressed as

$$\dot{\gamma} \simeq k\frac{\sigma}{\eta_0 n \langle \ln H/H_0 \rangle} \tag{20}$$

In the equation n is, of course, the number of bonds transmitting the stress (and remaining unbroken). As the sample continues to be sheared, so the stress will fall until n has reached its equilibrium value. The exact shape of the stress vs. time curve will depend upon the distribution of the bond strengths and the viscosity of the continuous phase. There are two corollaries of this. If the distribution of bond strengths is infinite, such as a log-normal distribution, which is a distribution not infrequently occurring in natural circumstances, the apparent viscosity will tend to become infinite as the shear rate decreases to zero, whilst at the other end of the scale it will asymptotically approach a finite value. Though the simple theory outlined above does not embrace this condition when all the bonds are broken and the rate of shear is such that none is able to reform, the asymptotic value must be the same as that given by the hydrodynamic theory when all the particles are discrete.

If, on the other hand, there is a finite lower limit to the bond strengths, a certain minimum force will be required to break these bonds before any continuous flow is possible. The material will exhibit a yield value and thereafter an apparent viscosity which decreases with increasing shear rate.

It is possible to extend the network theory a little further. The preceding discussion has related solely to adventitious chains of individual particles. If the particles have any tendency to flocculate, as is commonplace in colloidal dispersions, the degree of aggregation will depend on the size and number of the suspended particles. In a suspension of a very large number of very small particles, aggregation is essentially complete before the particles have had time to migrate towards any centres of aggregation; the result will be a more or less uniform distribution of single particles. If the aggregation proceeds slowly, that is, although the volume concentration of suspended particles is the same, the particles are larger and therefore less numerous, an inhomogeneous structure may form, consisting of a number of aggregates. Neighbouring aggregates may then be joined by chains of single particles, often several chains between each pair. The effect of this is to modify the network theory. The number of chains now supporting the tensile force is equal to the number of aggregates multiplied by the average number of chains joining the aggregates. If this modification is inserted, the theory will now predict an enhanced dependence of the elastic component and the maximum stress overshoot on the dispersed volume fraction.

To sum up, it has been shown that, whether the principal controlling factor affecting the flow of the more concentrated suspensions be the hydrodynamic interference with the path of the particles or the attractive interactions between the particles, the general effect of increasing the concentration is first to increase the viscosity, then for the observed viscosity to become dependent on the applied shear rate, for some elasticity to appear, and finally for other phenomena such as stress overshoot to occur. All this applies to a suspension of rigid particles. The two approaches should not be regarded as antagonistic. It is highly likely that the true situation for any suspension combines some aspects of both. This will become clearer when the properties of some typical food materials are discussed later. If the particles are flexible a different situation obtains. By consideration of the hydrodynamic conditions alone, it is evident that flexible particles are likely to become entangled and the resulting entanglements may have very different properties from those of the chains or the enmeshed rigid rods so far discussed. The properties of suspensions of flexible particles have been extensively studied by polymer scientists and the theory expounded in the standard works on high polymers. It is not proposed, therefore, to discuss it further here.

Starting with simple liquids and adding increasing amounts of matter in suspension, a picture has been built up showing a range of properties from pure Newtonian liquid flow to non-Newtonian flow, viscoelasticity and yield value. These all comprise what has been called 'fluid' properties. Hydrodynamic considerations are the ultimate controlling influence. When, however, the structure within the material takes over as the controlling factor, any deformation will be finite, however long the stress may be applied. Increasing the stress does not result in a transformation to flow conditions, but may eventually lead to fracture when the stress exceeds the cohesiveness of the sample. These are the materials which are said to exhibit 'solid'-type behaviour. The proper approach to any theory of their properties is by the methods of structural mechanics. If any liquid phase is present, it occupies the voids in the solid structure. Its contribution to the rheological properties arises from the fact that, as the structure is deformed under the action of the stress, the liquid will be constrained to set up local flow patterns. Some energy will be used up in this process and this will depend on the rate at which the structure deforms. The liquid will exert a damping effect on the deformation and the solid will become viscoelastic. The magnitude of the effect will necessarily depend not only on the properties of the liquid, but also on the nature of the solid structure. If that structure be an open lattice, then the liquid may flow fairly freely and the damping will be small. If, on the other hand, the structure is a porous one consisting of fine interconnecting capillaries, then the viscous forces may be large and make a substantial contribution to the overall pattern of behaviour.

The distinctions between the different types of behaviour are by no means clear-cut. As always in the field of rheology, there is a blurring of the edges. It is not always easy to pin-point the exact point of transition from fluid to solid or from lattice to capillary. An example of this continuous transition will be given later in Chapter 11 when the development of the structure of cheese is discussed.

CHAPTER 4

Some Empirical Models

In Chapter 1, some models, which were called 'architectural' models, were discussed and it was shown how they could be used to describe some of the behaviour of viscoelastic materials. It was suggested that other types of models exist, which purport to simplify the description of some rheological behaviour. These are usually encountered in the field of fluid flow, where their function is to describe the shape of experimentally determined flow curves in a manageable number of parameters.

In the previous chapter it was shown that it can be predicted that a liquid, which on its own is Newtonian, will show non-Newtonian behaviour on the addition of a second component. Even in this simple case, though, the expression for non-Newtonian behaviour is not exact, except for the most dilute additions. When further components are added, and interactions between particles and between particles and the liquid all occur, the situation becomes much more complicated. It is just this situation which the food rheologist frequently encounters. His materials often contain several ingredients and their distribution in size and shape may not be capable of precise specification. In these circumstances, any attempt to synthesize a mathematical expression for the non-Newtonian behaviour he observes is hardly likely to be rewarding. The use of empirical models then comes into its own. Essentially these are phenomenological descriptions of the flow curves. A few of the most frequently used models will be mentioned here and their merits and shortcomings will be discussed briefly.

Undoubtedly, the model which appears most frequently in the literature is the power law model. The constitutive equation for this is

$$\tau = k\dot{\gamma}^\alpha \qquad (21)$$

where k is a constant sometimes referred to as the consistency index and α may have any positive value. When α is greater than unity the material becomes less fluid as the shear rate increases. This is known as shear-thickening, or sometimes as dilatant. The latter term is not to be recommended as it also has another connotation in physics and the two properties do not necessarily coexist. When α is less than unity it is known as shear-thinning or sometimes pseudoplastic. When α is 1, of course, we get the flow curve of a Newtonian liquid. The three cases are shown in Fig. 12, in which are drawn curves for $\alpha = 1\cdot5$, $1\cdot0$ and $0\cdot5$ respectively.

It is sometimes more convenient to work in terms of the apparent viscosity. Equation (21) then becomes

$$\eta' = \tau/\dot{\gamma} = k\dot{\gamma}^{\beta} \tag{22}$$

where β has been written for $\alpha - 1$. Now, β is positive when the material is

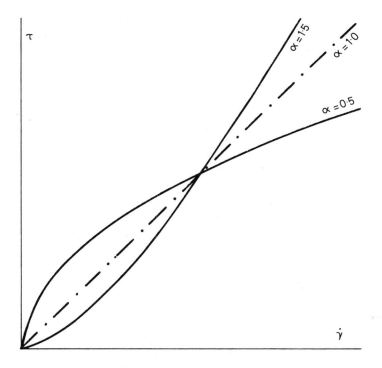

Fig. 12. Flow curves for power law liquids.

shear-thickening and negative when it is shear-thinning, whilst k is seen to be the viscosity at unit shear rate.

In this form, some of the limitations of the power law model become apparent. Consider first the shear-thinning case. One can see that since β is negative, as the shear rate increases towards infinity, so the viscosity tends towards a value of zero, whilst at the other extreme, as the shear rate decreases towards zero, the viscosity tends to become infinite. The latter may be regarded as plausible if the network theory elaborated in the previous chapter is accepted and there is a distribution of bond strengths reaching right down to zero. However, an apparent viscosity of zero is most unrealistic. Common sense suggests that, however high the shear rate, the viscosity should not fall below that of the continuous medium.

An even more serious objection is to be seen when one examines the physical dimensions of the equation. As has already been pointed out, if the equation is to have any physical sense, it must be dimensionally homogeneous and the constant of proportionality, if it be a true physical property, should have dimensions which are independent of the material whose property it is describing. The power law fails in this respect. The mathematical implication is also open to criticism. Stress and rate of flow are vector quantities. If the stress be reversed, then the rate of flow should be reversed equally and uniquely. It may be simpler to consider the reciprocal effect, i.e. of reversing the flow. If $\dot{\gamma}$ is replaced by $-\dot{\gamma}$, the new equation becomes

$$\tau' = k(-\dot{\gamma})^\alpha$$

Since α is generally a fraction, it may be written as α_1/α_2 where α_1 and α_2 are integers. If α_1 is even, it can be seen that τ is always positive, whilst if α_2 is even, τ is imaginary. So that, as α varies between 0 and 1, the value of τ oscillates between real and imaginary and between positive and negative. The equation is therefore said to be unstable.

Notwithstanding these serious objections on theoretical grounds, the power law equation has found wide use as a means of expressing the flow behaviour of many non-Newtonian fluids in terms of only two parameters. Moreover, if logarithms of the viscosity and shear rate are plotted, the equation reduces to a straight line. This enables the character of the material to be recognized instantly, as well as facilitating the calculation of the parameters. Provided that it is always borne in mind that it is only an empirical way of manipulating the numbers obtained when making rheological measurements, its simplicity has much to recommend it. Furthermore it will be shown later that, in some cases, the fit of the experimental data to this law is remarkably good and may apply over quite wide ranges of stress and shear rate. These points have been deliberately laboured at some length. Reading through many papers in which shear-thinning data are reported, one often finds that the results are quoted in the form of the constants of the power law. In the event this may well be acceptable, but it would often appear that it had been assumed as axiomatic that the law would apply. The only justification for using the law is the pragmatic one that it fits the data better than any alternative and when it does so, it facilitates interpolation.

Another arbitrary mathematical model for shear-thinning fluids was proposed by Steiger and Ory. They added a single term to the basic Newtonian equation to allow for the curvilinear nature of the flow curve, viz.

$$\dot{\gamma} = a\tau + c\tau^3 \tag{23}$$

Once again we have an equation which is unacceptable on dimensional grounds. a has the dimensions of a fluidity (the reciprocal of viscosity) but the dimensions of the constant c, although comprising integral powers of mass, length and time, are quite unrecognizable as representing any likely physical property. On the other hand, it will be observed that it allows properly for the reversal of sign and to that extent is analytically stable. However, if the expression is considered purely from the point of view of the algebra, it will also be observed that whilst it expresses the stress uniquely in terms of shear rate, the converse is not strictly true. If the equation be rewritten as a cubic in τ, i.e.

$$\tau^3 + \frac{a}{c} \cdot \tau - \frac{\dot{\gamma}}{c} = 0$$

we have an equation which possesses three roots. As long as a and c are both positive, as they must be by definition, only one root is real and this is the value with which we are concerned in practice, so that the analytical objection is not any real impediment to its use. On the other hand, it will be obvious that this equation cannot be adapted to describe shear-thickening behaviour. A negative value of c quickly leads to a decreasing shear rate as the stress increases when that stress exceeds $(a/3c)^{1/2}$! The Steiger and Ory equation is thus seen to be less versatile than the power law.

A comparison of these two two-parameter equations shows that a material which obeys the power law will break down progressively with increasing shear rate throughout any shear rate range, whereas the Steiger and Ory equation would predict a more or less constant viscosity at low shear rates, with the breakdown increasing more rapidly as the shear rate increases. Both ultimately lead to the absurdity of a zero viscosity as the shear rate becomes infinite. The range of application of either is thus limited to regions well away from infinite shear rate, and due care must be taken when using them not to attempt an interpretation which implies an extrapolation beyond the range of the measurements. Their greatest merit is that it is only necessary to determine two parameters. The arithmetic is simple and the closeness of fit of the data to the proposed model can easily be calculated using elementary statistical methods.

Let us now consider a more plausible situation in which the material is characterized by two viscosities, one the viscosity at infinitely low shear rate, which we will denote η_0, and the other the viscosity which occurs when any structure is completely broken down, the viscosity at infinitely high shear rate, η_∞. The viscosity at any intermediate shear rate may be presumed to be the result of partial breakdown due to the shear and this can be expressed in a general equation of the form

$$\frac{\eta_0 - \eta}{\eta_0 - \eta_\infty} = f(\dot{\gamma}) \tag{24}$$

This equation is perfectly general and can be applied to any material whose viscosity changes with shear rate. It is not necessary at this juncture to go into any discussion of the value of the function $f(\dot{\gamma})$. If it were known exactly, there would be no further need of any models. There have been several attempts to derive this function theoretically. All of them have, at some stage, involved simplifying assumptions. It is often a matter of personal choice whether one regards these assumptions as sufficiently plausible; as yet there is no consensus in this matter. For the present purposes, therefore, we may regard all the proposed variations of this model as empirical.

With even the simplest function it becomes necessary to employ three parameters to describe the curve, the two limiting viscosities and one parameter from the function $f(\dot{\gamma})$. As a consequence, fitting the model to any experimental data becomes that much more difficult than with the two-parameter models. There are several requirements·which the function must fulfil. If the expression is to be dimensionally homogeneous, it is evident that the function must be a pure numeric. In order to achieve this, $\dot{\gamma}$ must always be associated with a multiplying factor, which we may call λ, which has the dimensions of a time. Furthermore, if the expression is to be valid for flow in either direction, only even powers of $\dot{\gamma}$ may appear in it.

The simplest form that the expression can take is

$$\tau = \eta_0 \frac{1 + (\lambda_1 \dot{\gamma})^2}{1 + (\lambda_2 \dot{\gamma})^2} \dot{\gamma} \tag{25}$$

As long as λ_1 is less than λ_2 the value of η falls monotonically from the zero shear rate viscosity η_0 to a lower infinite shear rate viscosity $\eta_0(\lambda_1^2/\lambda_2^2)$. The expression was originally proposed by Reiner to explain the shape of the flow curves which Ostwald had obtained for many colloidal solutions he had examined. Ostwald had distinguished only two different regions, possibly because he was unable to make measurements at sufficiently low shear rates to observe any lower constant viscosity region. He called the region in which the viscosity appeared to be breaking down as the shear rate increased, the structural region, and the upper one, where the flow curve had become essentially linear, the laminar region. Later, Oldroyd was to study, both theoretically and experimentally, some polymer solutions which showed similar phenomena, but which he observed also possessed elastic properties. From the more general and more sophisticated model he proposed, it is possible to derive exactly the same eqn (25), so this will be referred to as the simplified Oldroyd model. Although this model successfully describes a material's behaviour when the viscosity is finite at both the low and high shear rate extremes and is therefore more easily credible than the two-parameter models described above, it does have one serious drawback. It is self-evident that, whatever may be the mechanism by which the structure of a material changes when measurements are being made, any increase in shear rate should accompany an increase in stress. Equally, the converse is true: if the stress is increased, the shear rate must increase. Otherwise the system is unstable. The algebraic expression of this statement is that, whatever the values of $\dot{\gamma}$, τ must be monotonic and $d\tau/d\dot{\gamma}$ must be positive. If the simplified Oldroyd model is examined, it will be seen that these criteria can be met only if λ_2/λ_1 is less than 3. If we put this in terms of practical experience, the maximum reduction in viscosity which can occur as a result of shear is to one-ninth of the original (infinitely low shear rate) viscosity. If this model be used for a material whose viscosity breaks down by more than this amount, then it would predict that in the middle of the range the rate of breakdown is greater than the rate of increase of shear rate and in this region the stress which the material can support should decrease as the shear rate increases. The model in this form can be applicable only to those materials which exhibit only a modest degree of breakdown under shear. Once this limitation is accepted, the model takes up a useful place in the repertory of the rheologist. It enables him to describe a flow curve in terms of two readily identifiable physical properties: the limiting viscosities, which may indeed be experimentally accessible, and a characteristic time, which is in fact just the reciprocal of the shear rate at which half of the structural breakdown has occurred.

Let us now turn to the plastic materials, those which will not flow until a certain minimum stress is applied. A large number of these are encountered in the food industry. The simplest possible model that can be conceived for this type of material is the Bingham plastic. In this model it is assumed that, once the minimum stress (the yield stress) has been exceeded, the excess gives rise to normal Newtonian flow. It is also assumed that the immobile nature of the material is immediately and completely recovered once the stress falls below the yield value. This may be expressed as

$$\tau = \tau_0 + \eta_B \dot{\gamma} \qquad (26a)$$

This form is not algebraically satisfactory and the full expression should be

$$|\tau| = |\tau_0| + \eta_B |\dot{\gamma}|, \, (|\tau| > |\tau_0|); \qquad \dot{\gamma} = 0, \, (|\tau| \leq |\tau_0|) \qquad (26b)$$

The reason for this apparently pedantic nicety will become evident when the question of combining the mathematical models and practical measuring systems is discussed in Chapter 5.

The Bingham model is not very useful because few actual materials are found which behave in such a simple manner. More often, even when the yield point is precisely determinable, the flow thereafter is non-Newtonian. It is hardly surprising that one of the most popular modifications of the Bingham model is to insert the power law for the viscous component. This gives the Herschel and Bulkeley model:

$$\tau = \tau_0 + k_{HB} \dot{\gamma}^\alpha \qquad (27)$$

The same stricture on algebraic rigour also applies to this equation and, indeed, to all the yield value models. The Herschel and Bulkeley model has the merit that it describes a flow curve in a small number of parameters and often is found to give a reasonably good representation of an experimentally determined curve. It does, however, suffer from the disadvantage that, unlike the simple power law, it is less easy to fit to the observed data as it usually involves an extrapolation in order to arrive at the value of τ_0.

An ingenious variation was devised by Casson for use with suspensions of pigments. Making some more or less plausible assumptions about the

behaviour of elongated particles which form chains, he derived a formula
which may be written

$$\tau^{1/2} = \tau_{CA}^{1/2} + \eta_{CA}^{1/2} \dot{\gamma}^{1/2} \tag{28}$$

where τ_{CA} and η_{CA} are usually known as the Casson yield value and the
Casson viscosity respectively. It is noteworthy that this equation is
dimensionally homogeneous and that it does not require the apparent
viscosity to tend to zero when the shear rate becomes very large as does the
Herschel and Bulkeley equation. In fact it predicts that the apparent
viscosity approaches asymptotically to the Casson viscosity. It has one
practical shortcoming in that the agreement between the theoretical curve
and experimental data is often least good just where it might be expected to
be at its best—in the region just above the yield point. However, this will
be considered more fully later. For many practical purposes it has the great
merit that it enables a flow curve for a plastic material to be described in
only two parameters which are easy to comprehend. As a result it has a
considerable following in some branches of the food industry. Whether
one ascribes to it any theoretical significance or merely regards it as a
convenient empirical relation depends on whether one is prepared to
accept Casson's original premises. It is a matter of some interest, yet quite
paradoxical, that some of the substances for which the equation appears to
fit the experimental data best, are fairly densely packed suspensions of
amorphous particles, where the conditions are least like those postulated
by Casson.

For the purpose of extrapolating towards the yield stress from measurements made at low shear rates, it matters little which of these two models is
used. It is only as the shear rates become higher that the two diverge
appreciably. This is clearly shown in Fig. 13, where the stress and shear rate
have been plotted on a logarithmic scale. Each curve has been calculated
on the basis of the sample having a yield stress of 10 Pa and an apparent
viscosity at unit shear rate of 20 Pa s. The exponent for the Herschel and
Bulkeley equation has been given the value $\frac{1}{2}$. It can be seen that below a
shear rate of 1 s^{-1} the curves are practically indistinguishable. The Casson
equation has the undoubted advantage that since only two independent
parameters are involved, these are easily calculated from any experimental
data.

Neither the Herschel and Bulkeley nor the Casson equation allows for
any elastic behaviour in the material. One model which does indeed allow
for this is the simplified Oldroyd model. The form given in the earlier

paragraph applies only to the equilibrium condition of steady flow. In the unsteady state, when the stress is varying, the equation takes the form

$$\tau + \sigma_1 \dot{\tau} = \eta_0(\dot{\gamma} + \sigma_2 \ddot{\gamma}) \tag{29}$$

The mathematically minded will see that eqn (25) is a particular solution of this equation. This equation will be encountered again when the behaviour of a material in the viscometer is discussed.

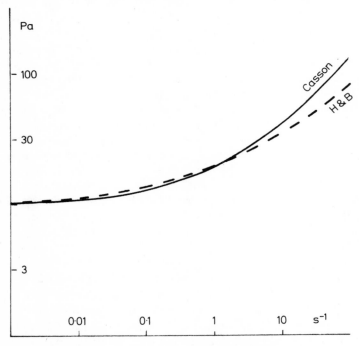

FIG. 13. Flow curves for yield value models.

There is no limit to the number of further complications which can be thought up, using the various simple models as a starting-point. Occasionally one comes across published papers in which an experimentally observable pattern of behaviour has been described by means of quite complicated models. It may be taken as a general precept that the more complicated the model, the less useful it becomes. Usually it is unlikely to be profitable to consider any more sophisticated models than those described in this chapter.

CHAPTER 5

The Measurement of Rheological Properties

In the preceding chapters we have indulged in what we may call 'armchair rheology'. We have considered only the properties of materials in the abstract and in terms of some mathematical models which may be useful in describing those properties. But food rheology is a practical science and contemplation alone will not solve all its problems. We must now turn our attention to the practical side and consider some of the problems involved in the measurement of those properties. These are essentially mechanical properties—they involve the movement of matter. It is an interesting observation that one often finds in Russian literature that the use of the word 'rheological' is avoided; instead, these properties are termed 'structure-mechanical'. In spite of the clumsiness of the term, it is a very useful concept: it underlines the fundamental truth that the properties with which we are concerned are mechanical and that they arise as a result of the structure of the material being studied. The means by which the properties may be studied all involve mechanical action; the properties cannot themselves be measured in isolation. In most cases what is observed is the performance of an instrument when the sample is contained within it. In one case—the flow of liquids through a capillary—it is the converse which applies: then what is observed is the behaviour of the liquid when confined within the measuring apparatus. In either case the principle is the same. The actual observations made in that process which is called 'measuring the rheological properties' are observations of the interaction between the samples and the measuring apparatus. The properties themselves can only be inferred from the nature of this interaction. This point cannot be too strongly stressed. Most experienced rheologists will be well aware how important it is to bear this in mind when undertaking taste panel or other sensory tests, where the interaction between sample and tester is observed

51

subjectively, but it is easy to overlook it when the 'tester' is an inanimate piece of apparatus. The only difference is that in our case it is possible to give (in theory at least) precise mathematical expression to the performance of the apparatus, whereas when human judgement is the only observation, such quantification is not available to us.

Before proceeding to consider specific instruments or real materials, we may consider the basic principles which may be used in rheological instrumentation. From the discussion of the basic ideas it will be evident that the common requirement for any measurement is that there shall be a stress and an associated movement, whether that movement be continuous flow, in the case of a liquid sample, or a limited strain, as in the case of a solid sample. It is immaterial from the point of view of the theory whether the stress be applied and the movement observed, or the sample be constrained to move and the required stress be observed. The action, by which term we include either the application of a stress or the constraint to move, may be constant or varying, unidirectional or oscillating. It will now be obvious that some of the models described in the previous chapter will not be appropriate in every case, the criticisms levelled at them there underlining the restrictions which they must impose on any theoretical treatment of the interaction between instrument and sample.

Measuring instruments will, as a generic term, henceforth be called rheometers. However, when the sample is liquid, the commoner though etymologically less precise term 'viscometer' will be used. Leaving aside those rheometers which work on an *ad hoc* principle and have been developed, perhaps in the context of a particular product, to give an empirical indication of that product's acceptability, rheometers may be divided into two main types. In one, relative motion takes place between two opposing surfaces of the apparatus. The motion may be tangential, in which case shear is applied, as in a concentric cylinder viscometer, or normal, in which case the sample is either compressed or extended. In the other type the sample is contained within the walls of an open-ended vessel and the relative movement takes place between the axial part of the sample and that in contact with the walls. The capillary viscometer is the archetype for all in this category. The physical principles invoked are identical in both cases, but because of the different configurations the algebraic treatment is necessarily different.

Let us consider the second type first. In accordance with the principles laid down in the opening paragraphs, only the case of a cylindrical tube will be considered. Tube viscometers are, in fact, almost always cylindrical. The engineer who wishes to use the rheological data, too, will usually be

THE MEASUREMENT OF RHEOLOGICAL PROPERTIES

concerned with flow in pipes, though occasionally he may have to consider flow in open channels, which may have any number of different cross-sections. The derivation of the Poiseuille equation for the steady flow of a Newtonian liquid through a capillary tube is given in any textbook on viscometry. We may now modify it, but retaining the same arguments, to derive equations for the steady flow of some non-Newtonian liquids.

In every case we start with the same three basic premises. Assuming that the liquid flows along a tube whose radius is r and length l, by virtue of a pressure difference P between the ends, the shear rate and stress on any cylindrical surface within the sample at a radius x from the axis are given by

$$\dot{\gamma} = -\frac{du}{dx}, \tau = \frac{Px}{2l} \tag{30}$$

where u is the velocity of the liquid (relative to the walls of the tube) at that radius.

With these two must be combined the constitutive equation describing the flow behaviour of the liquid:

$$\tau = f(\dot{\gamma})$$

In the case of the Newtonian liquid this is, of course, the linear relationship defining viscosity:

$$\tau = \eta\dot{\gamma}$$

For the first example, let us substitute the power law. The constitutive equation is now

$$\dot{\gamma} = k\tau^{\beta} \tag{22}$$

The first step is to evaluate the velocity u at any radius x. Combining eqns (22) and (30) we get

$$\frac{du}{dx} = -k\left(\frac{Px}{2l}\right)^{\beta} \tag{31}$$

At the walls, $x = r$ and $u = 0$, so that

$$u = \int_{0}^{u} du = -\int_{r}^{x} k\left(\frac{Px}{2l}\right)^{\beta} dx$$

$$u = \frac{kP^{\beta}}{2^{\beta}l^{\beta}} \cdot \frac{1}{1+\beta}\left[r^{(1+\beta)} - x^{(1+\beta)}\right] \tag{32}$$

The second step is to calculate the volume passing through the tube in unit time. Let this be V. The volume dV flowing through an annulus of thickness dx and radius x is given by

$$dV = 2\pi x u \, dx \tag{33}$$

Therefore

$$V = \int_0^v dV = 2\pi \int_0^r xu \, dx = \frac{\pi k P^\beta}{2^\beta l^\beta} \cdot \frac{2}{\beta+1} \int_0^r \left[r^{(1+\beta)} - x^{(1+\beta)} \right] dx$$

Or

$$V = \frac{\pi k P^\beta}{2 l^\beta} \cdot \frac{1}{3+\beta} \cdot r^{(3+\beta)} \tag{34}$$

When $\beta = 1$, this reduces to the Poiseuille equation where k is the fluidity ($=1/\eta$). For any other value of β a single measurement is insufficient to define the liquid. At least two measurements with different values of P, l or r are necessary so that the equations can be solved for k and β.

An examination of the form of eqn (34) immediately suggests one possibility. If, instead of applying a steady pressure P, this pressure is continuously varied and the flow rate monitored, a plot of $\log V$ against $\log P$ will give a straight line with slope β as long as the liquid obeys the power law. This is the principle on which the Tsuda viscometer was based.

The same line of argument that was used to derive eqn (34) may be applied for any other model, by inserting the appropriate constitutive equation. If one considers the Steiger and Ory model and inserts eqn (23) into eqns (30), this leads to the expression

$$V = \frac{\pi P r^4}{8l} \left(a + c \frac{P^2 r^2}{6l^2} \right) \tag{35}$$

On the other hand, not every model leads to such simple results as these two. If we consider the simplified Oldroyd model, eqn (25), and rearrange it, it becomes a cubic in $\dot{\gamma}$:

$$\dot{\gamma}^3 - \frac{\lambda_2^2}{\lambda_1^2} \cdot \frac{\tau}{\eta_0} \cdot \dot{\gamma}^2 + \frac{1}{\lambda_1^2} \dot{\gamma} - \frac{\tau}{\lambda_1^2} \cdot \frac{1}{\eta_0} = 0 \tag{36}$$

If $-du/dx$ is substituted for $\dot{\gamma}$ and $Px/2l$ for τ as before, whilst in theory it is possible to solve this for u, the resulting algebraic expression is so cumbersome as to become unwieldy. It is not practical, therefore, to attempt to evaluate the constants for the simplified Oldroyd model from capillary flow data. The converse does not necessarily hold. If the numerical values of the constants are known, it is easy to calculate the velocity profile in the tube for any given pressure and hence to arrive at a figure for the volume flow.

The examples just given are all of true, though non-Newtonian, fluids. Under some circumstances, materials exhibiting a yield value may also flow in a tube. When the stress in the neighbourhood of the walls, i.e. the stress given by the value $\tau = Pr/2l$, is greater than the yield stress, some flow will take place. The material near the walls will flow according to the behaviour predicted by the model being considered. The central core, though, that is, that part of the sample whose radius r_c is less than the critical value given by $\tau_0 = Pr_c/2l$, will not exhibit shear flow, but will move solidly as a plug, with a velocity equal to that of the material at that critical radius.

In order to arrive at an expression for the total flow through a tube when the material has a yield value, it is necessary to consider the flow of the central core and of the peripheral region separately.

In the case of the Herschel and Bulkeley model, the velocity at any point in the sheared region may be arrived at in the same way as in the power law fluid example above, but substituting the expression $(Px/2l) - \tau_0$ for $Px/2l$. From this we may deduce that the velocity at the radius where the shear rate falls to zero is given by

$$u = \frac{2l}{P\left(1 + \dfrac{1}{\alpha}\right)} - \frac{1}{k^{1/\alpha}}\left(\frac{Pr}{2l} - \tau_0\right)^{(1+1/\alpha)} \tag{37}$$

and the whole of the sample within the cylinder bounded by this radius moves forward at this velocity. The cross-sectional area of this plug is

$$\pi r_c^2 = \frac{4\pi l^2 \tau_0^2}{P^2} \tag{38}$$

so that the volume per unit time moving with plug flow is given by

$$V_{\text{plug}} = \frac{8\pi l^3 \tau_0^2}{P^3\left(1 + \dfrac{1}{\alpha}\right)k^{1/\alpha}}\left[\frac{Pr}{2l} - \tau_0\right]^{(1+1/\alpha)} \tag{39}$$

The volume rate of flow in the outer, sheared, region may be evaluated as before but now integrating only between the limits $x = r$ and $x = r_c$. This gives

$$V_{\text{sheared}} = \frac{8\pi l^3}{P^3\left(3 + \dfrac{1}{\alpha}\right)k^{1/\alpha}}\left[\frac{Pr}{2l} - \tau_0\right]^{(2+1/\alpha)}\left[\frac{Pr}{2l} + \frac{\left(4 + \dfrac{1}{\alpha}\right)}{\left(2 + \dfrac{1}{\alpha}\right)} \cdot \tau_0\right] \quad (40)$$

The total rate of flow is the sum of these two equations (39) and (40).

Similar arguments can be used to derive expressions for the velocity field and the total volume flow for the Casson model, leading to only marginally less involved formulae. The expressions obtained for the volume flow rates of the different models have been brought together in Table 1 and some typical velocity profiles have been drawn in Fig. 14. To enable them to be compared they have all been based on the same volume flow rate through a capillary the ratio of whose length to diameter is 50.

Table 1. The flow of various model fluids through tubes

Model	Volume flow rate
Newtonian fluid	$\dfrac{\pi P}{8\eta l} \cdot r^4$
Power law	$\dfrac{\pi P^{1/\alpha} k}{2^{1/\alpha}\left(3 + \dfrac{1}{\alpha}\right)l^{1/\alpha}} \cdot r^{(3+1/\alpha)}$
Steiger and Ory	$a \cdot \dfrac{\pi P r^4}{8l} + c \cdot \dfrac{\pi P^3 r^6}{48l^3} = \dfrac{\pi P r^4}{8l}\left[a + c \cdot \dfrac{P^2 r^2}{6l^2}\right]$
Herschel and Bulkeley	$\dfrac{8\pi l^3}{P^3 k^{1/\alpha}}\left[\dfrac{Pr}{2l} - \tau_0\right]^{(1+1/\alpha)}\left[\dfrac{P^2 r^2}{4l^2} \cdot \dfrac{1}{\left(3 + \dfrac{1}{\alpha}\right)}\right.$
	$\left. + \dfrac{Pr\tau_0}{l}\dfrac{1}{2 + \dfrac{1}{\alpha}} \cdot \dfrac{1}{3 + \dfrac{1}{\alpha}} + 2\tau_0^2\dfrac{1}{1 + \dfrac{1}{\alpha}} \cdot \dfrac{1}{2 + \dfrac{1}{\alpha}} \cdot \dfrac{1}{3 + \dfrac{1}{\alpha}}\right]$
Casson	$\dfrac{\pi P r^4}{8\eta_{CA} l}\left[1 + \dfrac{8}{3}\dfrac{l\tau_0}{Pr} - \dfrac{2^{9/2}}{7}\dfrac{l^{1/2}\tau_0^{1/2}}{r^{1/2}P^{1/2}} - \dfrac{16}{21}\dfrac{l^4\tau_0^4}{r^4 P^4}\right]$

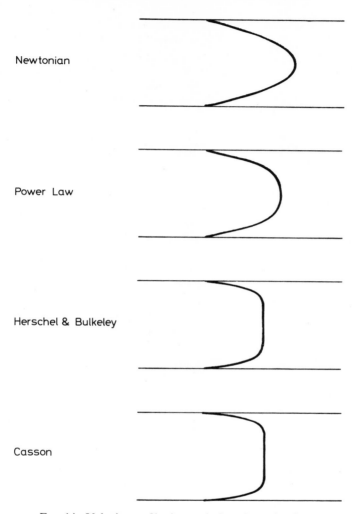

Newtonian

Power Law

Herschel & Bulkeley

Casson

FIG. 14. Velocity profiles in steady flow through tubes.

It is obvious from the foregoing considerations that the viscometry of non-Newtonian materials using the flow through capillary tubes is generally unlikely to be rewarding except perhaps when the departure from Newtonian behaviour is minimal. It is not possible to obtain a flow curve which is characteristic of the material by direct measurement, as the shear rate and stress never occur explicitly in the expressions for flow. On the other hand, if some plausible model is assumed, then it may be possible to calculate some material parameters if more than one experiment is carried out with tubes of different dimensions or with different applied pressures. However, the equations are not always easy to solve. On the other hand, the equations are very useful from the point of view of the use of rheological data. If an appropriate model can be chosen, then the equations can be used to estimate the flow through any pipe. The significance of these equations when there is any yield value may be especially stressed. The ratio length to diameter is particularly important. In the examples of Fig. 14, the pressures calculated to maintain the same volume flow for the Newtonian case and the two yield value models were very similar; yet had the tube been only twice as long, the yield stress would never have been exceeded. The flow of the Newtonian liquid would have been reduced to half, but that of the materials with a yield value completely inhibited.

Let us now consider the other type of viscometer, the two-boundary viscometer, in which the sample is sheared between two surfaces. These vary considerably in the shape of the sample contained between the effective surfaces. This is sometimes loosely referred to as the 'geometry' of the system. The principle, however, is always the same. A mechanical action is applied to one of the surfaces and the resulting reaction is observed directly.

The ideal situation would be one in which the sample were sheared between two perfectly plane parallel plates. However, as has already been seen, it is sometimes necessary for the sample to be sheared continuously for a considerable time, so that the total strain may be quite large, before an equilibrium condition is reached. To achieve this with a linear arrangement would require an instrument with at least one dimension inconveniently long. Prototype instruments of this type have been constructed for particular purposes in research laboratories, but none is a practical commercial proposition. The instrument designer's solution is to replace the linear motion with rotary motion. In this configuration the two boundaries are virtually infinite in the direction of motion and the sample may be continuously sheared as long as one wishes. This arrangement results in a compact instrument, which can be made very economical also in terms of sample size. Nevertheless, in achieving this, some sacrifice has to be made. Rotary motion may give rise to secondary flows in other directions within the sample, in addition to any which may arise because of the particular properties of the sample material. For the present purposes these secondary flows will be ignored and the treatment will concentrate on the effects in the direction of the applied action only. This is unlikely to be a serious limitation from the point of view of the food scientist who wishes to measure rheological properties. For this, the ideas developed in the following paragraphs will be adequate. However, the engineer wishing to use the results of the measurements in the design of industrial plant would be ill-advised to overlook those forces that may develop perpendicular to the direction of flow. Although these are usually second-order effects, they are not necessarily insignificant. The more important consideration for our purposes is the fact that the simple relation between stress and shear, which characterizes the sample and which would be observed directly were it possible to use linear motion, now has to be modified to take account of the geometry of the viscometer.

In the first place, we shall consider the equilibrium condition when the action is unidirectional and constant. This is, for instance, the condition when a steady reading is obtained on a rotational viscometer. Let us consider the sample in the annular space between two concentric cylinders. As before, the theoretical deduction of the relation between the torque on the cylinders and the relative motion between them may be found in any elementary textbook and we shall proceed by using the same lines of reasoning, but adapting them to take account of the non-Newtonian behaviour of our samples. The assumption is made that the torque required to cause one cylinder to rotate is transmitted without loss to the other cylinder, that is, there is no storage of energy within the material in the intervening space and none is dissipated as heat.

The shear stress within the sample, at any radius, is given by

$$\tau = \frac{\Gamma}{2\pi r^2 l} \tag{41}$$

and the shear rate by

$$\dot{\gamma} = r \cdot \frac{d\omega}{dr} \tag{42}$$

Consider first the power law model, with its constitutive equation

$$\tau = k\dot{\gamma}^\alpha \tag{21}$$

Combining these three equations we get

$$\dot{\gamma} = r \cdot \frac{d\omega}{dr} = \left[\frac{\Gamma}{2\pi r^2 lk} \right]^{1/\alpha} \tag{43}$$

The relative angular velocity between the two cylinders is given by

$$\Omega = \int_{r=r_1}^{r=r_2} d\omega = \frac{\alpha}{2} \left(\frac{\Gamma}{2\pi l} \right)^{1/\alpha} \frac{1}{k^{1/\alpha}} \left[\frac{1}{r_1^{2/\alpha}} - \frac{1}{r_2^{2/\alpha}} \right] \tag{44}$$

which may be rewritten

$$\Gamma = 2\pi l \left[\frac{2}{\alpha} \left(\frac{1}{r_1^{2/\alpha}} - \frac{1}{r_2^{2/\alpha}} \right)^{-1} \right]^{\alpha} \cdot k\Omega^{\alpha} \tag{45}$$

where r_1 and r_2 are the radii of the inner and outer cylinders respectively. So, the equation connecting the torque and the angular velocity associated with it is of exactly the same form as the constitutive equation for the model.

In order to construct a flow curve for the sample from the experimental observations of torque and velocity of rotation, it only remains to find the relation between angular velocity and shear rate. Eliminating Γ from eqns (43) and (45) gives

$$\dot{\gamma} = \frac{1}{r^{2/\alpha}} \cdot \frac{2}{\alpha} \left[\frac{1}{r_1^{2/\alpha}} - \frac{1}{r_2^{2/\alpha}} \right]^{-1} \cdot \Omega \tag{46}$$

This equation gives the relation at any radius and shows that the shear rate varies across the annulus. Moreover, this variation depends not only upon the dimensions of the annular space, but also upon the properties of the material filling it. There is no unique value of shear rate which may be related to the angular velocity and it becomes necessary to decide on what is an appropriate value to use which will enable the torque–angular velocity curve best to represent the stress–shear rate curve. The German Industrial Standards organization (DIN), having considered the various alternatives available, recommends the use of the arithmetic mean of the shear rates at the two cylindrical surfaces when calculated for a Newtonian fluid. This is defined as the representative shear rate. By analogy, the shear stress at that radius at which that shear rate occurs is defined as the representative stress.

Substituting the radii of the two cylinders in eqn (46) above, we get for the Newtonian case ($\alpha = 1$)

$$\dot{\gamma}_{r_1} = \frac{2}{r_1^2} \left[\frac{1}{r_1^2} - \frac{1}{r_2^2} \right]^{-1} \cdot \Omega, \quad \dot{\gamma}_{r_2} = \frac{2}{r_2^2} \left[\frac{1}{r_1^2} - \frac{1}{r_2^2} \right]^{-1} \cdot \Omega \tag{47}$$

whence

$$\dot{\gamma}_{rep} = \frac{1}{2}\left(\dot{\gamma}_{r_1} + \dot{\gamma}_{r_2} \right) = \left(\frac{1}{r_1^2} + \frac{1}{r_2^2} \right)\left(\frac{1}{r_1^2} - \frac{1}{r_2^2} \right)^{-1} \cdot \Omega$$

or

$$\dot{\gamma}_{rep} = \frac{r_2^2 + r_1^2}{r_2^2 - r_1^2} \cdot \Omega \tag{48}$$

The radius at which this occurs is given by

$$\frac{1}{r_{rep}^2} = \frac{1}{2}\left(\frac{1}{r_1^2} + \frac{1}{r_2^2} \right) \tag{49}$$

i.e. the representative radius is the root harmonic mean square of the two cylinder radii. It is a common practice for manufacturers of commercially available viscometers to calibrate their instruments to read these representative values.

For the present we will accept that this calibration is a reasonable approximation for many purposes and for many materials as long as their departure from Newtonian behaviour is not too great. But it is clear that it is impossible for the angular velocity–torque curves to represent equally well all flow curves. Whilst the exponent α is given explicitly, as long as the sample conforms to the power law model, the values of the consistency index will be only approximate. The departure from exactness and its implications will be considered later, in Chapter 6, when the subject of accuracy is discussed.

If we apply the same mathematical procedures, but substituting instead of the power law the Steiger and Ory model, eqn (23), in eqns (41) and (42), we arrive at the expression

$$\Omega = \frac{a\Gamma}{4\pi l}\left[\frac{1}{r_1^2} - \frac{1}{r_2^2} \right] + \frac{c\Gamma^3}{48\pi^3 l^3}\left[\frac{1}{r_1^6} - \frac{1}{r_2^6} \right] \tag{50}$$

Again, this is of the same form as the original constitutive equation and the constants a and c can be readily evaluated.

The simplified Oldroyd model, as before, leads to less simple mathematics. The constitutive equation, arranged as a cubic in γ, is

$$\dot{\gamma}^3 - \frac{\tau}{\eta_0}\left(\frac{\lambda_2}{\lambda_1} \right)^2 \dot{\gamma}^2 + \frac{1}{\lambda_1^2}\left(\dot{\gamma} \right) - \frac{\tau}{\eta_0} \cdot \frac{1}{\lambda_1^2} = 0 \tag{51}$$

As before, we may substitute eqns (41) and (42), but the solution of the equation, though algebraically straightforward, becomes a mathematical exercise and will not be considered further. Suffice it to say that it is again a cubic and of similar form to the original constitutive equation.

So far it has been shown that, provided that the material between concentric cylinders is liquid, the general form of the equation connecting the applied torque and the relative motion of the cylinders is similar to the equation of the model proposed. When the material has a yield value it is necessary to distinguish several different conditions. Let us consider, in the first place, the case when the action is the application of a stress. Until the torque exceeds a certain minimum value, no motion will take place. As before, the torque may be written

$$\Gamma = 2\pi r^2 l\tau \qquad (52)$$

and it will be seen that putting $\tau = \tau_0$ (the yield stress), the condition that any flow takes place in the material is

$$\Gamma > 2\pi r^2 l\tau_0 \qquad (53)$$

This has its lowest value at the surface of the inner cylinder, where $r = r_1$. Therefore flow commences when $\Gamma > 2\pi r_1^2 l\tau_0$. However, only that part of the material nearer the inner cylinder for which the torque is greater than $2\pi r^2 l\tau_0$ will flow: it is not until the torque exceeds the value given by $2\pi r_2^2 l\tau_0$ that all the material will be in a state of flow. There will therefore be three distinct regions in the torque–rotation curve. At the lower end this will have the form $\Omega = 0(\Gamma \leq 2\pi r_1^2 l\tau_0)$ and is of no further interest. What is of interest is the point at which rotation commences, as this is determined by the yield stress and the curve for higher values. If, on the other hand, the action is an applied relative motion, then it follows that, in at least part of the material, the yield stress must be exceeded and only the two upper regions of the curve are observable. Put another way, when the cylinders are at rest, the torque is indeterminate. The two upper parts of the curve will be considered separately.

Let us take, in the first instance, the simple plastic model for which the constitutive equation is

$$\tau = \tau_0 + \eta\dot{\gamma} \qquad (54)$$

When $\tau > \tau_0$ at the outer cylinder we may substitute for τ and $\dot{\gamma}$ and integrate to obtain the expression

$$\Omega = \frac{\Gamma}{4\pi\eta l}\left[\frac{1}{r_1^2} - \frac{1}{r_2^2}\right] - \frac{\tau_0}{\eta} \ln \frac{r_2}{r_1} \qquad (55)$$

which we may rearrange to read

$$\Gamma = 4\pi l \left[\frac{1}{r_1^2} - \frac{1}{r_2^2} \right]^{-1} \left[\eta\Omega + \tau_0 \ln \frac{r_2}{r_1} \right] \tag{56}$$

Comparing this with the relation established for a purely viscous liquid, it is seen that the effect of the yield stress is to move this part of the curve a distance proportional to τ_0 and $\ln(r_2/r_1)$ in the direction of the Γ-axis, whilst the slope remains unchanged. From the practical point of viscometry, the viscosity may be obtained directly from the slope and a knowledge of the viscometer constants, whilst the yield stress can be calculated from the intercept obtained by extrapolating this part of the curve to the Γ-axis. When, however, the torque is less than $2\pi l r_2^2 \tau_0$, this expression does not apply as only part of the sample is sheared. The lowest speed of rotation at which the expression is valid may be obtained by substituting $\Gamma = 2\pi l r_2^2 \tau_0$, whence

$$\Omega_0 = \frac{\tau_0}{2\eta} \left[\left(\frac{r_2}{r_1} - 1 \right) \left(\frac{r_2}{r_1} + 1 \right) - 2 \ln \frac{r_2}{r_1} \right] \tag{57}$$

If r_2/r_1 is only slightly greater than unity (i.e. the distance between the cylinders is small compared with their radii), we may expand the expression within the brackets in ascending powers of $h = r_2 - r_1$, giving

$$\Omega_0 = \frac{\tau_0}{\eta} \left[h^2 - O(h^3) \right] \tag{58}$$

which shows that the critical rotation speed increases approximately as the square of the distance between the cylinders.

When $\Gamma < 2\pi l r_2^2 \tau_0$, the rotational velocity is less than the critical velocity and only part of the material is sheared. The maximum radius at which any shear occurs is given by r_0 when $\Gamma = 2\pi l r_0^2 \tau_0$. Substituting this value for the outer limit in the integration gives rise to the expression

$$\Omega = \frac{\Gamma}{4\pi\eta l r_1^2} - \frac{\tau_0}{\eta} \left(1 + \ln \frac{\Gamma}{4\pi l r_1^2 \tau_0} \right) \tag{59}$$

A linear relation between rotation and torque does not hold in this region. The complete response curve then comprises a linear region along the axis $\Omega = 0$ up to the point given by $\Gamma = 2\pi l r_1^2 \tau_0$, then a curvilinear portion up to a point given by $\Gamma = 2\pi l r_2^2 \tau_0$, $\Omega = \Omega_0$, and a further linear portion, whose slope is proportional to the viscosity, above this. The difference between this response curve and the model is the appearance of the curvilinear portion where the model has a sharp discontinuity. The viscometer may be considered to have 'blurred the image' of the model.

The same reasoning may be applied to the other models which include a yield value. Taking only the Casson model as an illustration, let us consider first the condition when the yield stress is exceeded throughout the material. Inserting the values for the shear rate and stress in the model and integrating gives

$$\Omega = \frac{1}{\eta} \left\{ \frac{\Gamma}{4\pi l} \left(\frac{1}{r_1^2} - \frac{1}{r_2^2} \right) - \left[\frac{\Gamma}{2\pi l} \right]^{1/2} \left[\frac{1}{r_1} - \frac{1}{r_2} \right] \tau_0^{1/2} + \tau_0 \ln \frac{r_2}{r_1} \right\} \quad (60)$$

If we now insert for Γ the lowest value it can have for all the sample to be sheared, $2\pi l r_2^2 \tau_0$, we get for the corresponding rate of rotation

$$\Omega_{\text{crit}} = \frac{\tau_0}{\eta} \left[\left(\frac{r_2}{r_1} - 1 \right) \left(\frac{r_2}{r_1} - 3 \right) + 2 \ln \frac{r_2}{r_1} \right] \quad (61a)$$

Once again the critical rate of rotation depends on the yield stress, the viscosity and the ratio of the radii of the cylinders. For any value of angular velocity less than this critical value the sample will be incompletely sheared; there will be a stationary layer in contact with the outer cylinder and eqn (60) will not apply. The greatest radius at which shearing takes place is given, as before, by r_0, where $r_0 = 2\pi l r_0^2 \tau_0$. If the integration is now performed between the limits $r = r_1$ and $r = r_0$, the equation for the partially sheared material is obtained as

$$\Omega = \frac{1}{\eta_{\text{CA}}} \left\{ \left[\left(\frac{\Gamma}{4\pi l r_1^2} \right)^{1/2} - \left(\frac{\tau_0}{2} \right)^{1/2} \right] \left[\left(\frac{\Gamma}{4\pi l r_1^2} \right)^{1/2} - 3 \left(\frac{\tau_0}{2} \right)^{1/2} \right] \right.$$

$$\left. + \frac{\tau_0}{2} \ln \left(\frac{\Gamma}{4\pi l r_1^2 \tau_0} \right) \right\} \quad (61b)$$

The ratio of the radii of the cylinders no longer enters into the expression, it only serves to define the upper limit of the range of angular velocities for which the expression applies. As with the simple plastic model, the total response curve of the Casson model within concentric cylinders is in effect a blurred image of the model.

Qualitatively, the same reasoning may be applied to the Herschel and Bulkeley model. Apart from the portion of the curve lying along the

Γ-axis, the general solution for any value of the exponent α is not readily obtainable, except when $1/\alpha$ has integral values. From the practical point of view, the implication is that it is likely to be unrewarding to attempt to analyse an experimental response curve from a concentric cylinder viscometer in terms of the Herschel and Bulkeley model. Only the yield stress is reliably obtained.

From the preceding paragraphs it is evident that the shear rate varies across the gap in the viscometer in a manner which involves both the dimensions of the viscometer and the properties of the sample. When a sample flows through a capillary tube (Fig. 14), the shear rate always ranges from zero at the axis of the tube to a maximum at the wall, and the radial distribution of shear rates for any model always follows the form of the flow curve given by the constitutive equation for that model. In the case of the concentric cylinder viscometer, the situation is rather different. Figure 15 shows the distribution of shear rates across the gap in a viscometer in which the ratio of the radii of the cylinders (r_1/r_2) is 0·8. The same models have been chosen as in Fig. 14 except that, as the Herschel and Bulkeley model gives a distribution only marginally different from that given by the Casson model, it has been omitted this time. Instead, a second Casson model has been included, for a sample whose yield stress is three-quarters of that of the other. These have all been calculated for the same rate of rotation and the value of the shear rate given by the calibration, assuming that the viscometer had been calibrated in terms of representative values, is given on each diagram as a broken line. It is evident that, in the Newtonian case, there is considerable variation across the gap, the shear rate at the outer surface being only 0·64 of that at the inner surface. The variation is greater for the shear-thinning fluid, whilst it is quite dramatic when the sample exhibits a yield value, particularly when the yield stress is such that not all the sample is sheared. It is now obvious that, if the properties of the sample material are unknown, any torque measured in the viscometer cannot be referred to any specific value of shear rate.

Having seen that the interaction of concentric viscometers with various models increases in complexity as the models depart from simplicity, let us now consider the effects of enclosing the sample between two parallel plates which may rotate about their common axis. If the plates are separated by a fixed distance ($= d$, say), the shear rate at any point at a distance x from the axis is given by

$$\dot{\gamma} = \frac{\omega x}{d} \qquad (62)$$

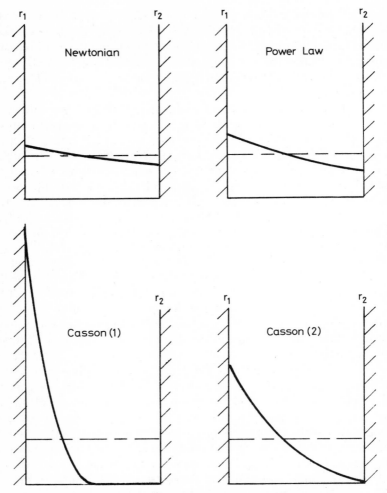

Fig. 15. Velocity profile across viscometer gap in steady flow.

The torque on an annular ring at radius x and of width $\mathrm{d}x$ is given by

$$\mathrm{d}\Gamma = 2\pi x^2 \tau \, \mathrm{d}x$$

where τ is the shear stress at that radius, whence

$$\tau = \frac{1}{2\pi x^2} \cdot \frac{\mathrm{d}\Gamma}{\mathrm{d}x} \tag{63}$$

Substituting these values of τ and $\dot{\gamma}$ in the appropriate model and integrating between the limits $x = 0$ and $x = r$ gives the total torque Γ directly. Of the true liquids, only the power law model gives a reasonably simple result:

$$\Gamma = \frac{2\pi r^3}{3 + \alpha} \cdot k \left(\frac{r}{d} \right)^{\alpha} \Omega^{\alpha} \qquad (64)$$

The exponent may, as before, be obtained directly from the experimental curve, but the constant k cannot be obtained independently of that exponent.

Turning now to materials with a yield value, a brief consideration of the mechanics of the system of two opposing circular plates shows that it is impossible for part of the intervening material to be sheared and part to be stationary. Accordingly, the intermediate condition which was evident in both tube flow and the flow between concentric cylinders is absent with this configuration. The solutions of the differential equations will apply to all the circumstances where the yield stress has been exceeded and there is relative motion between the plates. Consequently there will be no blurring of the pattern of behaviour. If there be a true yield stress it will give rise to a definite discontinuity at the point where flow commences. With either the Herschel and Bulkeley or the Casson model, the relation between the relative angular velocity and the torque is of the same general form as the relation between shear rate and stress, though the constants are modified. In each case there is a minimum torque below which shear does not take place. The two equations are:

Casson: $\qquad \Gamma = \dfrac{2\pi r^3 \tau_0}{3} + \dfrac{8}{7} \dfrac{\eta_{CA}^{1/2} \tau_0^{1/2} r^{7/2}}{d^5} \cdot \Omega^{1/2} + \dfrac{\pi \eta_{CA} r^4}{2d} \cdot \Omega \qquad (65)$

Herschel and Bulkeley: $\quad \Gamma = \dfrac{2\pi r^3 \tau_0}{3} + \dfrac{2\pi k r^{(3+\alpha)}}{(3+\alpha) d^{\alpha}} \cdot \Omega^{\alpha} \qquad (66)$

Finally, let us look at the interaction between the various models and the cone and plate configuration. At any radius x the tangential shear is proportional to the distance from the central axis and inversely proportional to the distance apart of the plates. If the apex of the cone just touches the plate at its centre of rotation, the shear must be independent of the radius, i.e. all the material between the cone and the plate is sheared identically. It follows that, as long as there is a unique relation between stress and shear for the enclosed material, the tangential stress on any point is also independent of the position of that point on the plate. The total torque on the plate is therefore given by

$$\Gamma = \frac{2\pi r^3}{3} \cdot \tau \tag{67}$$

and the shear rate by

$$\dot{\gamma} = \frac{r\omega}{d} = \Omega \cot \varphi \tag{68}$$

where φ is the angle between the conical surface and the plate and is equal to $(\pi/2) - \theta$, where θ is the semi-apical angle of the cone. Whatever model is used for the sample material, the relation between the rate of rotation and torque may be obtained by substituting directly the above values of τ and $\dot{\gamma}$ in the constitutive equation. Only the numerical values of the constants will be altered. For example, taking the Herschel and Bulkeley model,

$$\tau = \tau_0 + k\dot{\gamma}^\alpha \tag{27}$$

$$\frac{3\Gamma}{2\pi r^3} = \tau_0 + kr^\alpha \cdot \cot^\alpha \varphi$$

$$\Gamma = \frac{2\pi r^3}{3} \cdot \tau_0 + \frac{2\pi r^3}{3} \cdot \cot^\alpha \varphi \cdot k\Omega^\alpha \tag{69}$$

τ_0 is directly determinable from the value of the torque at which flow commences or ceases and the diameter of the plate. The exponent and the consistency index are then readily obtainable from the remainder of the experimental data and the dimensions of the apparatus.

Up to this point only the interaction between flow characteristics and the configuration of different types of measuring instrument have been considered. Any elastic property which the sample may exhibit would not be observed under the equilibrium conditions which have been assumed. The route by which this equilibrium is achieved and the time taken to reach it will have been influenced both by the elastic and viscous properties of the sample and by the mechanical characteristics of the instrument. It follows that, by observing the behaviour of the viscometer before it reaches equilibrium, some information may be deduced about the elastic properties of the material. Three non-equilibrium conditions are commonly encountered. The first, already suggested in this paragraph, is the creep experiment in which a stress is applied and the consequent motion up to the attainment of equilibrium is studied. This has already been discussed theoretically in Chapter 1. The second is the converse of this in which a fixed strain is applied and the variation of the stress is followed up to the point of equilibrium. This is the stress relaxation experiment. In the third case, a variable stress or strain is applied and the ensuing non-equilibrium behaviour observed. This variable action is usually chosen to be alternating in form. A sinusoidal action of fixed period and amplitude is the most convenient as it leads to the simplest algebraic analysis. All three methods have been used successfully by food rheologists.

It will be appreciated that, when the measurement involves the use of apparatus whose moving parts have not attained equilibrium, in addition to the properties of the sample contained in it and the configuration of the sample space, the inertial properties of the moving parts of the apparatus will also have their influence on the behaviour that is observed.

Let us first consider the effect of applying a periodic motion to the driven surface of the viscometer. The problem to be solved is to find the amplitude and phase of the forced resonance of the opposing free surface. Conventionally, this free surface is supported by a friction-free torsional suspension, which provides the restoring torque. There are certain restrictions which must be placed on the model to be used for the sample material; the importance of the mathematical criticisms of some of them will now become obvious. Since the motion may be in either direction, of which either may be designated forward or reverse, only those functions which apply equally to either sign of the variables can appear in the equation of motion, i.e. $f(-\dot{\gamma})$ must $\equiv -f(\dot{\gamma})$ in the general equation $\tau = f(\dot{\gamma})$. This rules out such models as the power law, the Herschel and Bulkeley and the Casson models. Exceptionally, the power law could be admissible in the very restricted and particular case of the power being an odd integer. One is left mainly with the linear models and combinations of them.

Consider the forces acting on the free surface at any instant. There will be a restoring torque, acting in the opposite direction to that in which the surface is displaced from its rest position and proportional only to the torsional constant of the suspension and the angular displacement. There will also be a torque due to the inertia of the whole system which carries the surface and its acceleration. This will be in the direction of the displacement. The third contribution to the total torque will be the torque transmitted through the sample material due to the properties of the material and the relative displacement of the opposing surfaces. Since torque cannot accumulate at any surface, these three must be in continuous equilibrium and we may write this as a simple differential equation:

$$I\ddot{\theta} + \Gamma + K\theta = 0 \tag{70}$$

where θ is the displacement of the free surface from its rest position and I is the moment of inertia of the moving system. It only remains to insert the value of Γ appropriate to the combination of the model chosen to represent the sample and the configuration of the sample space and to solve the differential equation. This equation has been written in terms of torque and angular deflection because this is the way in which it is usually used in viscometry. It is, though, a perfectly general dynamic equation for the motion of a body, and could be equally applied to any linear viscometer. The full solution of the equation consists of two parts: one, the particular integral, which expresses the (dynamic) equilibrium or forced resonance condition; the other, the complementary function, which expresses the transient phenomena before the attainment of that resonance. Only the particular integral is of interest to the rheologist in the present context.

The transmitted torque may now be due to either the viscous or elastic properties or both. If the angular displacement of the driven surface from its median position is φ, the strain exerted on the sample will be proportional to the difference in angular displacement, $\varphi - \theta$. Any torque transmitted by reason of the elastic properties of the sample will at any instant be proportional to this difference, whilst any torque transmitted by reason of the viscous properties will be proportional to its first derivative, $\dot{\varphi} - \dot{\theta}$.

If we take as an example the cone and plate configuration and the Kelvin model, eqn (6), the strain in the direction of motion at any point is $(\varphi - \theta) \cot z$, where z has been written for the angle between the conical surface and the plate (instead of φ in eqn (68) to avoid confusion). Combining eqns (6) and (67) we get

$$\Gamma = \frac{2}{3}\pi r^3 \cot z [n(\varphi - \theta) + \eta(\dot{\varphi} - \dot{\theta}] \tag{71}$$

whence

$$I\ddot{\theta} + \frac{2}{3}\pi r^3 \cot z \cdot \eta(\dot{\theta} - \dot{\varphi}) + \frac{2}{3}\pi r^3 \cot z \cdot n(\theta - \varphi) + K\theta = 0 \tag{72}$$

If we now put

$$\varphi = \varphi_0 \sin \omega t$$

and write

$$\frac{2\pi r^3}{3} \cdot \frac{\cot z}{I} = C$$

the particular integral of this equation may be written in the form

$$\theta = \theta_0 \sin(\omega t + \delta)$$

where

$$\frac{\theta_0}{\varphi_0} = \frac{C(n^2 + \eta^2 \omega^2)^{1/2}}{\left[\left(C\eta\omega\right)^2 + \left(Cn + \frac{K}{I} - \omega^2\right)^2\right]^{1/2}} \tag{73}$$

and

$$\tan\delta = \frac{C\eta\omega\left(\frac{K}{I} - \omega^2\right)}{(C\eta\omega)^2 + Cn\left(Cn + \frac{K}{I} - \omega^2\right)} \tag{74}$$

θ_0/φ_0 is the relative amplitude of the free and driven members and δ the phase difference between them.

Consider first the behaviour of the system in the neighbourhood of resonance. If $K/I = \omega^2$, the relative amplitude becomes unity and the phase difference between the members becomes zero. But this is exactly the condition for the free oscillation of the free member in the absence of any medium between the plates. We may write for this value of the frequency $K/I = \omega_0^2$. When the driven plate has this frequency the response of the other one, once the dynamic equilibrium has been established, will be exactly synchronized with it and independent of any properties that the material in the sample space may have. However, putting $\theta_0/\varphi_0 = 1$, it can be seen that there is another, higher, frequency at which the amplitudes are again equal. This frequency, which we will denote by ω_1, is given by

$$\omega_1^2 = \omega_0^2 + 2Cn \tag{75}$$

The maximum amplitude will occur at some point between these two frequencies, actually at a frequency ω_m, such that $\omega_m^2 = \frac{1}{2}(\omega_0^2 + \omega_1^2)$. The value of the amplitude at this frequency will be given by

$$\left(\frac{\theta_0}{\varphi_0}\right)_m^2 = 1 + \left(\frac{n}{\eta}\right)^2 \frac{1}{\omega_0^2 + Cn} \tag{76}$$

This is the condition of forced resonance: the cone and plate are no longer in phase, the phase angle being

$$\delta_m = \sec^{-1}\left(\frac{\theta_0}{\varphi_0}\right)_m \tag{77}$$

Now let us consider what happens as we move away to frequencies well removed from the resonance region. At very low frequencies, putting $\omega \to 0$, the amplitude becomes constant and equal to $Cn/(\omega_0^2 + Cn)$, while the phase angle approaches zero—the plates are once again in phase. At the other end of the frequency range, as the frequency becomes very high compared with the natural frequency of the free member, it will be seen that the amplitude falls to zero while the plates become completely out of phase.

If, instead of the Kelvin model, we had chosen the Maxwell model, a somewhat similar result would have been obtained. As before, the free member executes oscillations of the same frequency as the driven member, but the relative amplitude is given by

$$\frac{\theta_0}{\varphi_0} = \frac{C\omega\eta n}{[\eta^2\omega^2(Cn + \omega_0^2 - \omega^2)^2 + n^2(\omega_0^2 - \omega^2)]^{1/2}} \tag{78}$$

and the difference in phase is given by

$$\tan\delta = \frac{n}{\eta\omega} \cdot \frac{\omega^2 - \omega_0^2}{(\omega^2 - \omega_0^2) - Cn} \tag{79}$$

Just as in the case when the sample material behaved according to the Kelvin model, the two members of the viscometer move with equal amplitude and in phase when the frequency is the natural frequency of the free member. Again there is a region whose frequency is just above this natural frequency, where the relative amplitude is greater than unity. Once again, as the frequency increases towards infinity, the amplitude decreases to zero. However, at the other extreme, the amplitude also falls to zero. Using the simplified Oldroyd model instead of the Maxwell model, exactly the same type of behaviour would have been observed, with the relative amplitude reaching a maximum greater than unity at some frequency higher than the natural frequency and falling away to zero at both zero and infinite frequencies.

Whilst, with the Kelvin model, both the maximum amplitude and the higher frequency at which it occurs are simply related to the properties of the sample and the dimensions of the apparatus, when the other models are used the relations are much less simple and are of little practical use if one wishes to evaluate any material constants from a curve obtained experimentally.

There is one interesting corollary to all these relationships. If the sample between the cone and plate should be Newtonian, any two frequencies, one above and one below the natural frequency, at which the amplitudes are the same are related to the natural frequency by the simple relation

$$\omega_{A1} \times \omega_{A2} = \omega_0^2$$

A consequence of this is that, if a curve be drawn of the relative amplitudes plotted against the logarithm of the frequency, the curve will be symmetrical about the natural frequency. On the other hand, if the sample is non-Newtonian this symmetry disappears. When any elastic properties are present, not only is the curve asymmetrical but there is a frequency range within which the amplitude of the free member is greater than the amplitude applied to the driven member. Here again, students of electrical theory will recognize the similarity with the magnification occurring in a resonant lumped circuit, but whereas the lumped circuit designer is more usually concerned with a large Q-factor and may be able to ignore the resulting small frequency shift, in the viscometric case only very small magnifications may be quite significant and any shift of the resonant frequency may be quite substantial.

Some curves have been drawn in Fig. 16, which show the typical shapes of the response when the sample can be represented by each of the models so far discussed. These curves have been drawn for samples such that, at the natural frequency of the viscometer, each would require the same (alternating) stress to produce the same alternating strain amplitude. The two viscoelastic models would further be indistinguishable at this frequency as the phase differences between stress and strain would be identical. Yet the response of the viscometer for these samples is strikingly different. This demonstrates how measurements made in the region of the natural frequency of the viscometer may serve as a sensitive test for any elasticity and its nature. If the sample has any permanent structure giving rise to its elasticity, then a Kelvin body type response may be expected, whereas if the elasticity be fugitive, then a Maxwell body type of curve will result.

Only simple linear models have been considered when the viscometer is in oscillatory motion as these are the only ones to which the above simple analytical procedure can be applied. The reason for the criticism of some of the proposed constitutive equations should now have become more

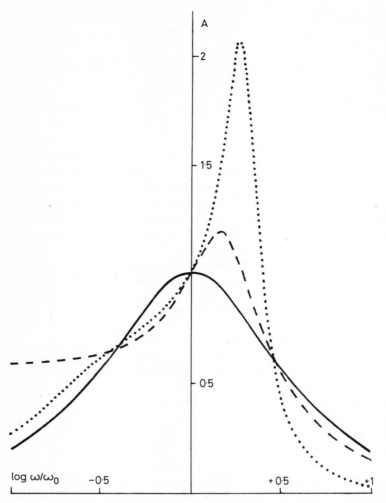

FIG. 16. Forced resonance in viscometer filled with model systems: ————,
Newtonian fluid; ———, Kelvin body; · · · · · ·, Maxwell body.

apparent. When, for instance, there is a yield stress, during every cycle
there will be two periods when the net torque, given by $I\ddot{\theta} + k\theta$, is
numerically less than that ($= \tau_0$) required to initiate flow, so that during
these periods there will be no shear and the members of the viscometer will
move with the same angular velocity. When the applied amplitude is very

small, it may be that this critical torque is never exceeded and the two members will move as one. At the other extreme, when the amplitude is very large, the synchronous periods may be very short and the free member may appear to move with simple harmonic motion. In between these two extremes the motion will be more complex.

In the last few paragraphs the motion of the free member of a viscometer has been considered in relation to the dimensions of the viscometer and the properties of the sample when those properties are described in the form of a simple model. If the motion is oscillatory, either because an oscillatory motion is applied externally to the other member, or because the free member has been displaced from its equilibrium position and is returning to it, the inertia of the moving system is also very important. It has been shown that the response observed is an inevitable consequence of the interaction of the viscometer's characteristics with the properties of the sample, and the two cannot be completely dissociated.

Let us now return to eqns (73) and (74). We may combine them and rearrange the result to write, putting A for the relative amplitude,

$$A\cos\delta = [(C\eta\omega)^2 + Cn(K/I - \omega^2 + Cn)][(C\eta\omega)^2 + (K/I - \omega^2 + Cn)^2]^{-1} \quad (80)$$

and

$$A\sin\delta = [C\eta\omega(K/I - \omega^2 + Cn)][(C\eta\omega)^2 + (K/I - \omega^2 + Cn)^2]^{-1} \quad (81)$$

When the natural frequency of the suspended system is very much higher than the applied frequency ($\omega_0 \gg \omega$), these may, to a close approximation, be reduced to

$$A\cos\delta = Cn[K/I + Cn]^{-1} \quad (82)$$

$$A\sin\delta = C\eta\omega[K/I + Cn]^{-1} \quad (83)$$

In the special case where the rigidity of the suspension is very great compared with any rigidity in the sample, the sample rigidity is proportional to that component of the amplitude which is in phase with the applied oscillations, whilst the viscosity is proportional to the out-of-phase component. This is the situation which is normally assumed for commercially available oscillatory viscometers. To arrive at it, it has been tacitly assumed that the amplitude measured is very small and that this amplitude is therefore a measure of the torque transmitted through the sample. Equations (82) and (83) show that this is not a necessary restriction. Even when the rigidity of the sample is significant compared with that of the suspension, the phase angle still gives the relation between the rigidity and the viscosity of the sample, but their absolute values can only be obtained by using the more exact formulae of eqns (82) and (83).

When measurements are made using oscillatory methods as just described, a slightly different notation is sometimes used. Writing $n^* = AK/C$, we get

$$(n^*)^2 = [n^2 + (\omega\eta)^2]$$

By analogy with dielectric theory and using the same convention that we are only concerned with the real part of the complex number, we may write

$$n^* = n' + jn'' \qquad (j = \sqrt{-1})$$

Before proceeding further, we must recall that eqns (73) and (74) were derived assuming the Kelvin body model, eqn (6). Earlier it has been shown that other models which can be represented by linear differential equations may also be used and these give rise to the same kind of response in the viscometer—a simple harmonic motion leading the applied motion in phase. At any one frequency the viscometer is unable to distinguish between the models. It can easily be seen by writing $\gamma = \gamma_0 \sin \omega t$ and eliminating τ and γ between eqns (6) and (9) that for sinusoidal oscillations the Maxwell and Kelvin models are readily interchangeable when

$$n_{\text{Kelvin}} \times n_{\text{Maxwell}} = \omega^2 \eta_{\text{Kelvin}} \times \eta_{\text{Maxwell}}$$

$$\frac{\eta_{\text{Kelvin}}}{\eta_{\text{Maxwell}}} + \frac{n_{\text{Kelvin}}}{n_{\text{Maxwell}}} = 1$$

It requires measurements to be made at more than one frequency to determine which model is appropriate. If n'' increases linearly with frequency the Kelvin model applies, whilst if it varies inversely with the frequency the Maxwell is appropriate. If any other pattern of variation of n'' is observed, then neither of these two models is appropriate.

One other type of oscillating motion may also be considered, that in which one member of the viscometer remains stationary throughout, but the free member is given an initial deflection and then allowed to swing freely. The interaction between the viscometer and the various model systems when using this mode of operation may be studied using the same theory as above, but replacing φ_0 by zero. In this case the steady state is never reached until the freely swinging member finally comes to rest. If the sample has no yield value, this rest position will, of course, be the same as the equilibrium position in the absence of a sample. If the suspended member comes to rest in any other position, then it may be inferred that there is a yield value. As will be shown later, it does not measure it. The important feature in this mode of operation is the way in which the equilibrium is reached from the original disturbed position. If the sample in the viscometer is a Newtonian fluid, this return to equilibrium may take place in two different ways, depending on the dimensions of the viscometer and the viscosity of the sample. If the moving system is overdamped, a condition which occurs when the viscosity is high, the moment of inertia of the free member is low, or the gap in the viscometer is small, the free member will return asymptotically to its rest position and the rate of decay will be less than exponential, the remaining deflection at any instant being given by

$$\theta = \theta_0 \exp(-pt)(\cosh qt + p/q \sinh qt) \qquad (84)$$

where p is written for $C\eta/2$ and q for $[(C\eta/2)^2 - \omega_0^2]^{1/2}$. If, on the other hand, the system is underdamped and this occurs when $C\eta < 2\omega_0$, that is, when the viscometer constant is small, the viscosity low or the moment of inertia of the moving member high, q in the above equation becomes imaginary. The expression in brackets may be replaced by $\cos \omega t + (C\eta/2\omega)\sin \omega t$, showing that the suspended member oscillates with a frequency less than its natural frequency in a free condition by an amount depending on the viscometer constant and the viscosity of the sample, whilst the amplitude of the oscillations decreases exponentially to zero.

As before, most models for non-Newtonian fluids do not lend themselves readily to a general treatment. The Kelvin model, however, is an exception. If the underdamped condition applies, the exponential decay still depends on the viscosity and is uninfluenced by the existence of any elastic property of the sample. However, this does affect the frequency of the oscillations, which may now be higher or lower than the free natural frequency and is given by

$$\omega^2 = \omega_0^2 + Cn - \frac{C^2\eta^2}{4}$$

The behaviour of the system when the sample has a yield value is of some interest. Although a simple algebraic solution is ruled out by the discontinuous nature of the stress–strain relationship, it is possible to make some qualitative predictions. When the free member is given its initial deflection, with the system at rest, the only driving force is the torque in the twisted suspension. When this is released, one of two things may happen. If this torque produces insufficient stress at the free surface to exceed the yield stress, i.e. $\Gamma - K\theta_0 < (2\pi r^3/3)\tau_0$, the system will remain at rest. However, if the yield value is exceeded, motion will commence, with an acceleration depending upon the viscosity of the sample and the excess torque available. Again we may split what ensues into two separate cases. In the overdamped case the motion will continue as above with a Newtonian fluid, but with the restoring torque reduced by the amount necessary to overcome the yield stress; the system will eventually come to rest when all that excess torque has been expended. In this rest position the suspended member will still be deflected towards the same side as i original deflection. In the underdamped case, when the position is reach where the torque on the suspension just matches that required to overcc the yield stress, the moving member will cease to accelerate but continue to be driven forward by virtue of its momentum until it come rest at the end of the first half-cycle, having followed the same path a Newtonian fluid but with the effective zero displaced by an amc necessary to compensate for the yield stress. This rest position at the en the half-cycle may, of course, be on either side of the rest position (θ = when the system is free. If, when the system comes to rest, the sto torque in the suspension is less than sufficient to overcome the yield str then this becomes the final rest position and no further motion ensues. deflection does not indicate the value of the yield stress, only its existe at some value corresponding to a greater deflection. If, on the other ha there is sufficient torque to initiate motion in the reverse direction, this take place, just as in the first half-cycle, but with the effective zero n switched over to the same side as the starting-point for this half-cycle. Oscillations may continue in this manner, with the effective zero alternating each half-cycle, until eventually the system comes to rest in a position where no further motion can be initiated. As before, the deflection in this position of rest is only an indication of the existence of a yield stress. Clearly the actual point at which this occurs will depend not only on the properties of the sample and the dimensions of the viscometer, but also on the amount of the initial deflection. The magnitude of the yield stress will determine only the range within which the rest position will occur. In Fig. 17 some curves have been drawn of displacement against time for the same hypothetical sample, showing how the oscillations progress after different initial displacements. These curves have been computed for a simple Bingham body and with initial displacements such that the torque in the suspension gave rise to stresses 2, 4, 6 and 8 times those required to overcome the yield stress. The deflection corresponding to the yield stress is indicated on the vertical axis. The only common

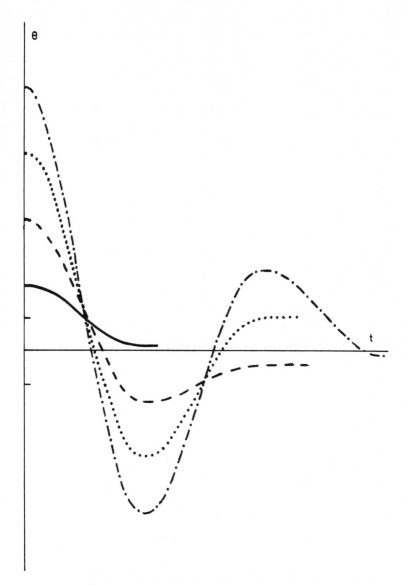

FIG. 17. Free oscillations in 'torsion pendulum' viscometer filled with a sample having a yield value, showing effect of initial displacement (see text).

feature of these four curves is that the final rest position is not at zero, but is such that the residual torque in the suspension cannot overcome the yield stress in the sample.

In the absence of a yield value and in the underdamped condition, the rate at which the oscillations decay, p in eqn (84), is proportional to the viscosity of the sample. The determination of that rate of decay provides a ready measurement of that viscosity. However, the various models for fluids whose viscosity is dependent on the shear rate do not give rise to simple solutions of the differential equation. If the rate of decay varies as the amplitude decreases, then this will give a qualitative indication of non-Newtonian behaviour, but this does not lend itself readily to the determination of any model parameters.

Let us now return to eqn (84). In the overdamped condition, i.e. when q is real, this represents the creep behaviour which ensues when a stress is suddenly applied to the sample and the stress relaxes as the sample material is sheared. Because of the interaction between the sample and the instrument, this is no longer either pure creep or pure relaxation. The actual motion of the free member of the viscometer which is observed is a function of the viscosity of the sample and the characteristics of the instrument. If we replace the Newtonian fluid by a viscoelastic material and represent this by means of the Kelvin model, the expression for the creep/relaxation now takes the form

$$\theta = \theta_0 \left[n + \frac{K}{C} \right]^{-1} \left[n + \frac{K}{C} \left(\cosh qt + \frac{p}{q} \sinh qt \right) \exp(-pt) \right] \quad (85)$$

where, as before, $p = C\eta/2$ but q is now $[p^2 - (Cn + K/I)]^{1/2}$. The motion is an exponential decay, asymptotically approaching a rest position in which the residual torque in the suspension of the apparatus is balanced by the energy stored in the sample, but its progress towards this position is retarded by a combination of the properties of the sample and the characteristics of the viscometer. Equation (85) is not particularly helpful, except that in the rest position, i.e. putting $t \to \infty$, it gives a value for the (Kelvin) rigidity explicitly, viz.

$$n = \frac{\theta}{\theta_0 - \theta} \cdot \frac{K}{C}$$

If we had substituted the Maxwell model for the sample instead of the Kelvin, this would have given rise to an even more cumbersome solution of the differential equation. In this case the rest position is that in which all the stresses have relaxed completely ($\theta = 0$). It is evident that, in this mode of operation, the instrument distinguishes between the solid-type model and the fluid type, but the actual determination of the material parameters requires a detailed analysis of the shape of the decay curve. Furthermore, it will be recalled that a sample with a yield value gives rise to a behaviour very similar to that of the Kelvin body; in each case the final rest position is taken up when there is a residual torque in the suspension and this position is approached by a retarded exponential decay. Similarly, the Newtonian fluid and the Maxwell body give rise to very similar patterns of retarded exponential decay to zero.

In the special case when the inertia of the moving system is small enough to be considered insignificant, eqn (85) may be simplified to read

$$\theta = \theta_0 \left[n + \frac{K}{C} \right]^{-1} \left[n + \frac{K}{C} \exp \left(- \frac{n + \frac{K}{C}}{n} \cdot t \right) \right] \qquad (86)$$

The final rest position is unaffected but it is now approached by a pure exponential, which again involves both the sample parameters and the instrumental constants. In a similar manner the creep/relaxation when the sample is described by the Maxwell model is an exponential decay to zero, with the decrement determined by the sample and instrumental parameters:

$$\theta = \theta_0 \exp \left[- \frac{t}{\eta} \left(\frac{1}{n} + \frac{C}{K} \right)^{-1} \right] \qquad (87)$$

It is only distinguishable from the Newtonian case by the fact that the rate of decay is slower by virtue of the presence of a rigidity.

Let us now consider the situation in which, instead of the applied stress being allowed to relax as the sample is sheared, this stress is maintained constant from the moment of application. We start with the same differential equation (70), but with the torque supplied by the suspension ($=K\theta$) replaced by a constant torque which we will call Γ_0. The solution of the equation, giving the displacement from the starting position for a Newtonian fluid, is now

$$\dot{\theta} = \frac{\Gamma_0 t}{IC\eta} [1 - \exp(-C\eta t)] \qquad (88)$$

and for the Kelvin model

$$\theta = \frac{\Gamma_0}{CnI} \left[1 - \exp(-pt) \left(\cosh qt + \frac{p}{q} \sinh qt \right) \right] \qquad (89)$$

where $p = C\eta/2$ and $q = [p^2 - Cn]^{1/2}$. These equations, as t tends towards infinity, become the standard viscometric equations—the Newtonian fluid reaches a steady dynamic equilibrium in which the shear rate depends only on the applied stress and the viscosity of the fluid, whilst the Kelvin body reaches a static equilibrium when the shear is proportional to the stress and inversely proportional to the rigidity of the sample. Equations (88) and (89) define the paths by which those equilibria are reached.

The equation for the Kelvin body may be looked at a little further. The ultimate displacement depends only on the ratio of the applied stress to that stored, as befits a solid-type model. However, the route by which this final equilibrium is reached may have one of three forms. In the over-damped case (q real), as before, the inertia of the instrument retards the approach to final equilibrium by an amount which involves both the parameters of the model and the characteristics of the apparatus. When the system is critically damped ($q = 0$), $(\sinh qt)/q = t$ and the expression becomes

$$\theta = \frac{\Gamma_0}{CnI}[1 - \exp(-pt)(1 + pt)]$$

This is particularly interesting as, whilst the ultimate displacement is uniquely determined by the rigidity, the route to it is controlled by the viscosity and the apparatus constants only. The rigidity does not enter into the exponential term. When q becomes imaginary, eqn (89) describes a situation where the motion combines an exponentially decaying creep with oscillations which themselves decay exponentially as the final value is approached. These three cases have been illustrated in Fig. 18. A curve has been computed for the same hypothetical sample and viscometer as was used for Figs. 4(a) and 16. This is drawn as a broken line in the figure. The displacement overshoots its final equilibrium position somewhat and then oscillates about it. This is a slightly underdamped situation. If the viscometer constant is increased or the moment of inertia of the moving system reduced, the critically damped situation may eventually be reached. In Fig. 18 the solid line represents the response for the same hypothetical sample when the moment of inertia is reduced by a factor of 2·2, which gives rise to critical damping. The viscometer constant is unchanged and the final equilibrium position is unaffected, but it is now approached asymptotically. A further reduction of the moment of inertia by the same factor gives rise to the overdamped response shown by the dotted line. Superficially the shapes of both the critically damped and the

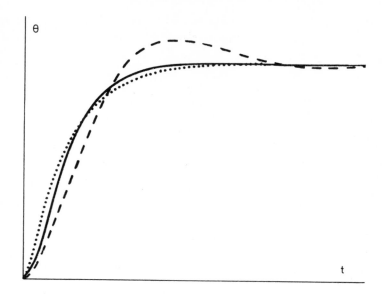

FIG. 18. Creep curve of a Kelvin body in an instrument having inertia: ----,
underdamped; ——, critically damped; ······, overdamped.

overdamped response curves resemble that of Fig. 4(a). The effect of
inertia in the apparatus on the time constant has already been noted. It will
also be observed that it reduces the acceleration in the early stages of the
creep, giving rise to a sigmoid curve.

A similar treatment may be applied to evaluate the interaction of the
instrument with any of the other models. In every case the effect of inertia
in the instrument is to modify the early stages of the creep curve most and
to introduce the possibility of an oscillatory motion should the system be
underdamped. In the critically and overdamped conditions the response
curve approximates to that of the pure model only as the elapsed time
becomes large compared with the characteristic time of response of the
instrument. The results will not be quoted, as they are in general too
cumbersome to be of practical value. One particular one is, however,
worthy of specific mention. The response curve for the standard linear
solid is

$$\theta = \frac{\Gamma_0}{Cn_b I}\left[1 - \exp(-pt)\left(\cosh qt + \frac{p}{q}\sinh qt\right)\right] \quad (90)$$

which is of exactly the same form as that for the Kelvin body. The only difference lies in the values of the constants p and q, which are now

$$p = \frac{C\eta_a}{2} \cdot \frac{n_a + n_b}{n_a}, q = (p^2 - Cn_b)^{1/2}$$

where the subscript a refers to the two-element arm and the subscript b to the single elastic element. The practical consequence of this is that a creep curve alone, obtained by means of an instrument which has significant inertia, cannot distinguish between these two models. Some additional evidence will be required in order to determine which is the more appropriate before attempting to analyse the curves.

The treatment so far has been developed from the point of view of what has been loosely called viscometry, although both liquid and solid models have been discussed. This has had considerable advantages in that it has enabled the theory to be kept simple. In a viscometer the sample dimensions and shape may be considered to remain constant however much it may be sheared. Moreover, in any rotation viscometer the length of the sample in the direction in which it is sheared is effectively infinite. Furthermore, it is possible to consider the unidirectional stress–strain relationships in isolation, without taking into consideration any force which may be generated normal to the direction of motion. However, the underlying ideas are perfectly general and may be applied to any form of rheological test. Instead of the sample being contained within a viscometer space and therefore constrained in its dimensions, it may be free-standing, say in the form of a rectangular or a cylindrical block. In this case it is more likely that the elongation or the compression of the block when a force is applied normally to one face will be measured. This is in contrast with the viscometric situation where the force is applied tangentially to produce a simple shear. In a perfectly simple isotropic material it may be assumed that any action resulting from the application of a force at any point is divided equally between the three mutually perpendicular directions, so that the linear displacement is one-third of that which would be expected had all the force been used up unidirectionally. For a perfectly elastic solid, this gives rise to the well-known relation that the Young's modulus is three times the modulus of rigidity. By analogy, the so-called elongation viscosity, sometimes known as the Trouton viscosity, is three times that value of the viscosity as determined by a simple shear measurement. All the above relations then, whether it be for forced oscillation, relaxation or creep, still apply, as long as the displacement is so small that it may be considered insignificant compared with the dimension of the sample in the direction of the applied action. When it becomes large enough to be significant, corrections must be applied to allow for this finite displacement. Usually it is sufficient to replace the linear displacement by the fractional displacement.

CHAPTER 6

The Reliability of the Measurements

It has been shown that rheological behaviour of real materials may be represented by various models and how these models perform when introduced into a theoretical viscometric space. It is now pertinent to consider the problem from the point of view of the instrumentation and to see just how reliable an instrumental measurement may be. If any rheological measurement is to be useful, it needs to be reliable. This can be achieved only if it is both precise and accurate. A measurement is regarded as precise when the spread of values which is obtained if it is repeated many times is so small as to be unimportant. Obviously the ideal for which one should aim is that every rheological measurement on a particular material should be identical, whoever makes the measurement and by whatever method. This is clearly an unattainable ideal, and it is of some importance to consider the extent to which actual practice may fall short of that ideal and to examine the factors which may contribute to that shortcoming.

Precision may be discussed under two headings, repeatability and reproducibility. These are not entirely independent. Conditions which are favourable for one are usually, though not necessarily, favourable for the other.

Repeatability is defined as the ability to obtain agreement when replicate measurements are made on the same, or an identical, sample, by the same instrument, as nearly as possible at the same time. It is thus a measure of the self-consistency of the measurements. The experimenter can determine it easily by making replicate measurements and it is usual to express the result in terms of the standard deviation of these replicates. It is generally more convenient if this standard deviation is expressed as a fraction of the mean value so that one can readily compare the relative importance of errors in measurements of different magnitudes. In its simplest form the repeatability is evidently dependent upon the satis-factory functioning of the instrument. However, we may assume that any rheometer used is free from malfunction and also that the operator is skilled in its use. There may still be reasons for departure from perfect repeatability. First, we must look at the sample. If the sample is of biological origin, as are many foodstuffs, it is possible that it may change with time, so that repeated measurements do not measure the properties of the same material. This also has another significance which, although not specifically connected with repeatability, it may be opportune to mention here. This state of affairs may impose a restriction on the range of rheological measurements which can be made. As an example, in the viscometry of dairy cream, if the measurements are made at low shear rates, the final equilibrium may not be attainable before the cream begins to deteriorate. For instance, if the shear rate is $10^{-3}\,s^{-1}$, it may take as long as $10^{5}\,s$, i.e. more than one day, for the breakdown under shear to reach a steady value, during which time it is almost certain that the properties of the cream will have changed substantially. Such a measurement is therefore not viable. A practical limit may need to be set that no meaning-ful measurements can be made at shear rates below, say, $10^{-2}\,s^{-1}$. In a similar manner, if a creep curve is being determined when the useful life of the sample, that is the length of time for which it may be expected to maintain its original properties, is limited, it is impossible to observe any retardation or relaxation phenomena which have time constants com-mensurate with, or greater than, this time. By a parallel argument, if the time which can be devoted to a measurement is limited by the experi-menter's patience or by the pressure on him to obtain results, there will be a limiting shear rate or creep rate below which he cannot possibly obtain useful measurements and this will depend upon the peculiar properties of his sample material.

To return to repeatability proper, another source of difficulty arises when the properties of the sample may be affected by the action of introducing it into the rheometer. Unless a standard procedure is adopted for each and every such operation, differences may appear in the measured properties which are not necessarily typical of the original but may have been engendered by the operator's action in introducing the sample. This problem is particularly troublesome when making measurements on materials such as pastes or doughs in a cone and plate viscometer. In setting the plates at the right distance apart, considerable work may be done on the sample and a long recovery period may be necessary for the sample to regain its original properties, if it ever does. If the sample needs to be reconstituted or prepared in any other way, then obviously it is of primary importance that the sample is as homogeneous as possible so that sub-samples shall be as near alike as possible. As a corollary to this, the size of the sample is important. Most food materials have several components and can never be homogeneous in the literal sense. The nearest approach is that one sample of material should be as nearly like any other sample as possible. The first requirement to be fulfilled is that the constituents shall be evenly distributed throughout the material. If the constituents have different sizes or, more probably, a range of sizes, then it is essential that the full distribution of sizes shall be adequately represented in the sample taken. This may impose severe limitations on the minimum sample dimensions acceptable. This may be most serious when a capillary viscometer or a cone and plate instrument is used. To take a numerical example, a cone and plate instrument may have a truncated cone such that the minimum separation between the plates is 80 μm, whilst at the periphery the separation may be 650 μm; a mayonnaise to be tested is an emulsion having discrete globules with diameters up to 35 μm, but relatively few of these, distributed throughout the material. It should be quite clear that in the regions of the sample space near the axis there is unlikely to be a representative proportion of the largest globules, but the probability will increase towards the outer edge. Armed with a knowledge of the distribution of the particle sizes and their effect on the properties of the material as a whole, it is theoretically possible to estimate the probability of any error due to the finite size of the sample. In practice the distribution may not be known and the effect will almost certainly not; indeed, it may be what is being investigated. One can only make a general statement, that there is likely to be some lack of repeatability because of inadequate sample size. In such cases it may well be necessary to com-promise. It may be decided to sacrifice some precision because of the advantages afforded by the cone and plate geometry. Or it might be decided to use a larger and more representative sample, if it is available, in the interest of the precision of the measurement, in a different type of instrument, when the measurement might be more difficult to interpret.

When the variation of one measured quantity with another is being studied, the precision of the measurement can be estimated from the scatter of the experimental points about the line obtained when the results are displayed graphically. The rheologist frequently determines a flow curve—the relation between the variables stress and shear rate—and in the execution of this, one or other is usually applied by some mechanical means and is assumed to be exact. The flow curve may then be determined as the statistically best-fitting line, either based on some preconceived model, or purely on the experimental evidence, perhaps as the best-fitting polynomial and the scatter calculated as a standard deviation about that line. This is patently analogous to an estimation of the repeatability. However, there is at least one potential source of scatter which is not evident if only true replicate measurements are made. If, in the course of the measurement, equipment ancillary to the rheometer is used to record the measured variable, this equipment will have its own characteristics. As an example, suppose the stress is measured by means of a transducer whose output is read on an analogue meter. A Class A meter may be guaranteed by the makers to indicate the true value to within, say, ±1% of the full-scale reading over all but the lowest 10% of its range and to have a linear response which is in keeping with this. It may be assumed that the meter is free from mechanical malfunction, so this may be taken as referring to the calibration of the scale. Provided that the limitations imposed by this specification are understood by the user, this order of precision is perfectly acceptable for many purposes. However, in the course of determining a flow curve, readings of the stress may be made over different parts of the scale. As a result of this, the relative (guaranteed) precision varies over the scale from ±1% of the reading at full-scale deflection to ±10% of the reading at one-tenth full scale. This lack of precision may have several consequences, which may be illustrated by some examples of actual measurements. Figure 19 shows a series of measurements made using a concentric cylinder viscometer with meter indication, the vertical lines indicating the extent of ±1% of full-scale deflection. Two lines have been drawn on this figure; both comply with the requirement that they pass within ±1% of full-scale deflection of every measured point. The broken line has been calculated as the linear regression line, having a standard deviation of about ±0·8 Pa about the line. This line would be consistent with the material being a Bingham plastic, with a yield stress of about 59 Pa. On the other hand the solid line corresponds to a power law fluid with an exponent of about 0·21. Whilst the latter line appears to be the better fit to the experimental data, because of the limitations of the precision tolerated by the specification, the evidence is not sufficient to justify making a firm choice between the two curves.

Sometimes the effect of meter tolerances shows itself only when it is necessary to change the scale factor. This may be effected either by using a different shunt or by a change of the gain of an associated electronic circuit. Then an apparent discontinuity in the flow curve may appear between consecutive points on either side of the change. Figure 20 shows the two

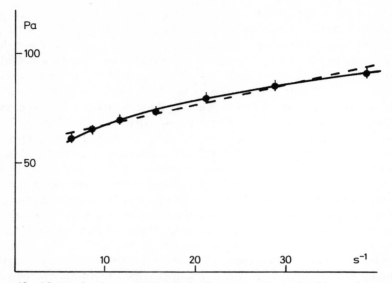

FIG. 19. Alternative interpretations of a flow curve determined by a viscometer with tolerances in calibration.

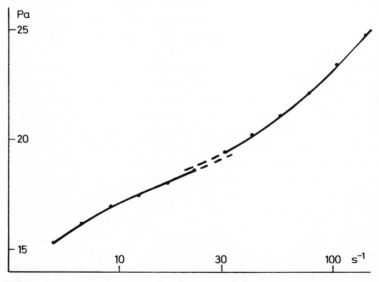

FIG. 20. Lack of continuity in instrumental readings through a change of scale factor.

portions of a flow curve obtained in this manner for a sample of a thickening agent. There is a clear discontinuity between the lower and upper portions. Solid lines have been drawn through the measured points and these have been extrapolated by the broken lines in the region where they should overlap. There appears to be a jump of about 0·3 Pa, but this could easily be accommodated by a tolerance of ±0·5 Pa on the upper portion and ±0·2 Pa on the lower, so that a single smooth curve could be drawn through all the data points. Furthermore, had only the upper or the lower portion of the curve been obtained, failure to allow for the instrumental tolerances could have led to a wrong interpretation of the behaviour of the sample.

Although the effect of ancillary equipment has been illustrated by examples based on meter readings, the same arguments apply to any part of the equipment. Some instruments incorporate a synchronous electric motor to provide a constant drive. The rate of revolution of these is not perfectly constant, but depends on the voltage and the frequency of the supply. In most developed countries, variations in the voltage are not usually sufficient to have a significant effect on the motor speed, but the frequency may fluctuate. Although this is usually statutorily controlled, certain variation is allowed, usually of the order of ±1% of the nominal value. The rheologist must therefore expect his shear rates to be subject to similar fluctuations. Whilst these may be expected most frequently to be gradual, the possibility of a sudden change, particularly during periods of high demand, should not be overlooked.

We have thus seen that some lack of precision in a rheological measurement may arise even though the equipment is guaranteed to be of a high quality. This is not to imply any criticism of the manufacturers of the instruments. Even the most skilled instrument-maker must permit himself certain tolerances within which to work. It is the responsibility of the rheologist to be aware of these tolerances, to familiarize himself with them and to take them into account when he attempts to draw any conclusions from his measurements.

While on the subject of ancillary equipment, it is opportune to consider the effect of temperature control. Foodstuffs vary considerably in the effect that temperature has on their properties. It is obvious that, to make reliable measurements on those which are very temperature-sensitive, the precise measurement and control of temperature is essential. In this connection it should be noted that thermometers, like other pieces of ancillary equipment, present some problems in precision. A good mercury-in-glass thermometer will normally retain its calibration with respect to its own zero for long periods of time unless subject to severe ill-usage. On the other hand, the glass creeps as it ages and this is reflected in a progressive shift in the calibration. Furthermore, temporary changes may be brought about through its use and the method of handling. The wise rheologist, therefore, should he wish to use such a thermometer, will always check its zero (i.e. its ice point) before use. Thermometers using semiconductor devices are probably no more stable than mercury-in-glass ones; the national standard offices are generally loth to approve of them, as they have not yet been sufficiently proved. Since they require additional electronic circuitry to give a temperature indication, they may be regarded as somewhat less precise indicators of temperature.

The effect of small errors in temperature control is most marked when a temperature coefficient is being measured. As an example, the viscosities of two mineral oils were determined using capillary viscometers at three different temperatures, nominally 20, 25 and 30 °C. For these relatively simple Newtonian liquids, the Arrhenius theory may be expected to apply and the plot of the logarithm of the viscosity against the reciprocal of the absolute temperature should result in a straight line whose slope measures an activation energy. The actual results of these measurements are plotted in Fig. 21. It will be seen at once that the three points for each oil are not collinear, but that there is about an 11% change of slope between the lower and upper halves of each curve. If the two outer temperatures had actually been 0·12 °C lower than the nominal and the middle temperature 0·12 °C higher, the linearity would have been near-perfect. If errors of just over a tenth of a degree in the temperature measurement can introduce errors of over 10% in the activation energy, it is suggested that to attain 1% precision the temperature control over a 5 °C range must be of the order of ±0·01 °C. When calibrated thermometers are used and the viscometer can be immersed in a water bath, as in the example just given, this is a perfectly reasonable requirement to meet. However, not all viscometers are so easy to control. In particular, when using instruments such as the cone and plate viscometers and compression-testing instruments, where the temperature control may depend upon external circulation and heated chambers, it may be most unreasonable to expect to achieve anything approaching this precision. In these cases one can only advise caution in the interpretation of any measurements made.

Reproducibility may be defined as the ability to obtain agreement on replicate samples when measurements are made at the same or different times, using different instruments or methods, perhaps in different laboratories. Thus, whereas repeatability is an internal comparison within a single system, reproducibility is the external comparison between systems. This can be assessed experimentally only by means of collaborative experiments. These are carried out from time to time in various contexts. Always it is found that agreement between instruments or methods is less good than the self-consistency of an individual instrument or method. Whilst all the factors that affect repeatability will affect the reproducibility in the same manner, there are also other factors to be considered. In the first place, the nominal replicate sample itself may be a

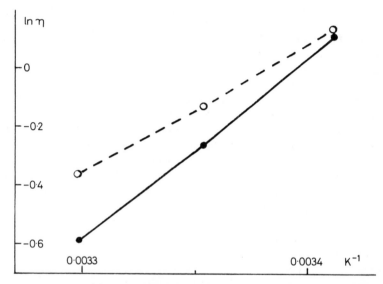

FIG. 21. Non-linearity, possibly attributable to errors in thermometry (see text).

source of difference. The rapid deterioration of some foods has already been referred to, but even those which are apparently more stable will nevertheless exhibit some change with time, although it may not be immediately obvious on casual inspection. A good example of this may be found in the ageing of butter or margarine. These are usually 'soft' immediately after manufacture, but set to their characteristically firm state within some hours and thereafter appear to preserve this state as long as the temperature remains constant. However, experiments have shown that the firming process is still continuing six months later. Samples of an otherwise identical product but of different age may be expected to have different rheological properties. As another example, in a recent collaborative experiment three samples of a gum solution were sent to different laboratories in sealed containers, to be examined there in viscometers of the same make and the same type. By the time the measurements were made the viscosities were all different, the highest measured value being about four times the lowest.

It is important, to ensure good reproducibility, that not only are the samples identical at their point of origin, but that their histories up to the time of measurement shall be identical. This includes not only the time factor, but also the effect of any temperature variation, agitation during transport, or exposure to varying degrees of humidity in materials which have any appreciable water activity. In many cases the samples must be prepared in some way before measurement. By an extension of the foregoing remarks it is easy to see that good reproducibility can be expected only if the method of preparation is standardized. There may even here be some hidden pitfalls. Every entrant in the local village show knows that no two Victoria sandwiches are alike, even though they may have been prepared from the same recipe. The difference may be due to the skill of the competitors, but may also be due to slight variations in the raw materials—often flour from a different wheat, eggs of a different age, butter from a different churn—or to slight differences in the actual temperature of the ovens. This is a trivial example, but it demonstrates the need for the method and the materials to be exactly and completely specified if reproducibility of sample preparation is to be achieved. Exactly the same argument applies to the rheologist, who cannot hope to reproduce another's measurements unless he be absolutely sure that both samples were prepared in precisely the same way. Moreover, the rheologist cannot use another's results for his own purposes unless he is completely satisfied with the identity of the samples. A natural corollary of this is that when a rheological measurement is made, on whatever material, the experimenter should record with it all the known details concerning the preparation and the history of the sample, as well as the physical conditions of the measurement. This is for his own use, should he later wish to refer to it, as well as for the benefit of others who may wish to use his data.

If the samples presented to the instrument are identical and all the conditions already described have been adhered to, the measurements should be as reproducible as they are repeatable provided that the instruments are correctly calibrated. In classical physics reproducibility and accuracy may be considered separately. Whereas reproducibility is concerned with comparisons among instrumental measurements, accuracy invokes comparison with some absolute standard. In the world of rheology this clear distinction becomes somewhat blurred. The usual method of achieving accuracy is by calibration. To the classical physicist this may seem so axiomatic that it does not need to be stated. However, it has already been demonstrated that, when dealing with rheologically interesting materials, the response of any instrument cannot be separated from the properties peculiar to the material. If a viscometer is calibrated, as it often is, by the use of a standard Newtonian fluid of known or predetermined viscosity, then its calibration can hold only for Newtonian fluids. Ideally, for use with a non-Newtonian fluid, it would be calibrated with one of similar characteristics. This, though, requires a knowledge of the very properties that are being sought. It is a circular argument and there is no way of breaking into it. One must therefore have recourse to calibration in terms of the fundamental units.

The fundamental quantities which are measured by a rheometer are usually a torque, if the motion is rotary, or a load if the motion is linear, and a velocity, again either angular or linear. These are simple physical quantities and there is no problem in calibrating any instrument so that these are accurately known. However, a knowledge of the torque or load and velocity are only a means to an end for the rheologist. In order to define the properties of his materials properly, he needs to establish the relation between stress and strain (Chapter 1, eqn (3)), and he requires his result to be uninfluenced by the instrumental means he uses to obtain it. Herein lies the problem of achieving accuracy. In the previous chapter it has been shown that it is the rule rather than the exception that the response of the instrument is conditional upon the properties of the sample material. Consequently, it is not possible to derive an unambiguous stress or strain to insert in eqn (3) simply from the observed load and displacement and the dimensions of the sample. Among the rotary instruments, only the cone and plate system allows this to be done. Even in this case, this is possible only in the sense of the stress and strain in the direction tangential to the motion to which we have restricted our arguments in the cause of simplicity. Stresses are set up in the other directions normal to that motion which we have chosen to ignore and which are dependent upon the properties of the material. In the linear mode, when a sample is contained between two parallel plates whose motion is restricted to tangential, then again the stress and strain may be evaluated uniquely, but currently no instrument using this principle is commercially available, though it is possible to adapt quite simply a compression instrument to perform this operation.

Let us return to the most popular viscometer, the concentric cylinders. It has already been shown (Fig. 15) that the shear rate across the sample is not a constant even when the sample is a simple Newtonian fluid, and the concept of a representative shear rate has been introduced (eqn (48)). It is now necessary to assume that the tangential stress is constant throughout the sample, i.e. that there is no differential accumulation of stress in any part of the sample. This is a reasonable assumption. It is possible from eqns (48) and (49) to calculate instrument constants to convert the angular velocity and torque into the representative shear rate and stress. These are the constants which are customarily given by commercial manufacturers for the calibration of their instruments, since they comply with an internationally recognized standard (DIN). As long as the sample material is Newtonian, the relation between representative stress and representative shear rate is an accurate description of the properties of the material. Let us consider what happens when the sample is not Newtonian. Since the same assumption must be made that there is no differential accumulation of stress, the stress calibration of the instrument will still hold and will give the correct value of the stress at the representative cylindrical surface (eqn (49)). However, the shear rate at that surface will no longer necessarily be correctly given by the instrumental calibration. It will depend upon the particular properties of the sample. To distinguish its value from the representative shear rate, let us call this the effective shear rate. To illustrate the difference we will take the case of a power law fluid, as this gives rise to the simplest mathematics. Putting in eqn (46) $r = r_{rep}$, from eqns (46), (48) and (49) we get

$$\frac{\dot{\gamma}_{eff}}{\dot{\gamma}_{rep}} = \frac{1}{\alpha} \cdot \frac{1}{2^{(1/\alpha-1)}} \left[1 - \left(\frac{r_1}{r_2} \right)^2 \right] \left[1 + \left(\frac{r_1}{r_2} \right)^2 \right]^{(1/\alpha-1)} \left[1 - \left(\frac{r_1}{r_2} \right)^{2/\alpha} \right]^{-1}$$

(91)

Table 2 gives the value of this ratio for selected values of the exponent α and ratio of the cylinder radii r_1/r_2. It is immediately obvious that for a shear-thinning fluid with $\alpha = 0.5$, the calibration is exactly correct. When α lies between 1 and 0.5, that is for a moderately shear-thinning fluid, the error in assuming that the representative shear rate and the effective shear rate are the same is small, particularly if the width of the annulus is small compared with the radii of the cylinders. However, with fluids which are more highly sensitive to shear rate, the error increases rapidly as they become more non-Newtonian. The practical implication is that if the flow

Table 2. Shear rate corrections for power law fluids between concentric cylinders

α \ P	1·00	0·95	0·90	0·85	0·80	0·75	0·00
2·0	1·000 0	0·999 7	0·998 6	0·996 7	0·993 9	0·989 9	0·707 1
1·5	1·000 0	0·999 8	0·999 2	0·998 1	0·996 4	0·994 0	0·839 9
1·2	1·000 0	0·999 9	0·999 6	0·999 2	0·998 4	0·997 4	0·935 4
1·1	1·000 0	1·000 0	0·999 8	0·999 6	0·999 2	0·998 7	0·968 2
1·0	1·000 0	1·000 0	1·000 0	1·000 0	1·000 0	1·000 0	1·000 0
0·9	1·000 0	1·000 0	1·000 2	1·000 4	1·000 8	1·001 3	1·028 7
0·8	1·000 0	1·000 1	1·000 3	1·000 8	1·001 5	1·002 5	1·051 1
0·7	1·000 0	1·000 1	1·000 5	1·001 1	1·002 0	1·003 3	1·061 4
0·6	1·000 0	1·000 1	1·000 4	1·001 0	1·001 8	1·002 9	1·049 9
0·5	1·000 0	1·000 0	1·000 0	1·000 0	1·000 0	1·000 0	1·000 0
0·4	1·000 0	0·999 7	0·998 6	0·996 8	0·994 0	0·990 3	0·883 9
0·3	1·000 0	0·998 6	0·994 3	0·986 7	0·975 6	0·961 0	0·661 4
0·2	1·000 0	0·994 8	0·978 4	0·950 5	0·911 7	0·863 5	0·312 5
0·1	1·000 0	0·969 3	0·880 8	0·752 7	0·610 5	0·475 8	0·019 5
0·05	1·000 0	0·865 7	0·578 9	0·325 4	0·165 9	0·080 4	0·000 0
0·0	1·000 0	0·000 0	0·000 0	0·000 0	0·000 0	0·000 0	0·000 0

curve obtained approximates to a power law, eqn (91) may be used to correct the representative shear rates and this is likely to be a sufficiently close approximation. When the departure from Newtonian behaviour is only modest, even this may be unnecessary except for the most precise work: the viscometer calibration in terms of representative values may be taken as sufficiently accurate. But what if the power law is not applicable? Unless there are any sudden discontinuities in the flow curve, it is usually safe to assume that $d\ln\tau/d\ln\dot{\gamma}$ is reasonably constant over short ranges of shear rate, such as are encountered within the annular gap; eqn (91) may still be applied, replacing α by $d\ln\tau/d\ln\dot{\gamma}$. In the power law, of course, $d\ln\tau/d\ln\dot{\gamma} \equiv \alpha$. This will provide a sufficiently accurate correction unless the viscometer gap is particularly large so that $d\ln\tau/d\ln\dot{\gamma}$ varies across it by a significant amount.

So far we have considered only the flow in the annular gap and assumed implicitly that this could be treated in isolation. But let us consider a real situation where the inner cylinder is completely immersed in the fluid contained in the outer. Figure 22 shows this in its simplest possible configuration. For the present we will simplify the argument by ignoring the fact that the flow field in the annular gap may be distorted near its edges. If it is the outer cylinder which is driven and the torque on the inner

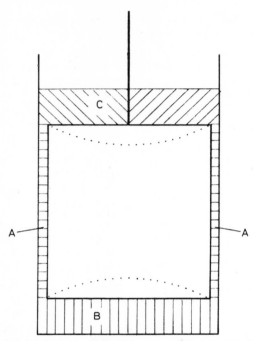

FIG. 22. Principal zones of shear in a concentric cylinder viscometer.

which is measured, we may consider three principal zones. There is the annular gap A, to which all that has been written so far applies. Between the base of the inner cylinder and that of the outer is zone B, which is in effect a parallel plate viscometer. Above the inner cylinder, in zone C, there is a third viscometer, in which torque is transmitted through the fluid from the upper part of the walls of the outer cylinder to the upper surface of the inner. The total effect of the three is for the torques to be additive.

If the viscometer is filled with a Newtonian fluid, the torque transmitted to the cylindrical surface, the base and the top of the inner cylinder will all be proportional to the angular velocity and the viscosity of the medium. The fact that the shear rates in the three zones will be different is of no consequence, as the viscosity is independent of shear rate. As long as the viscometer is consistently assembled so that the dimensions of the three zones are exactly the same every time, the additional torque on the ends of the cylinder will bear a constant relation to that on the cylindrical surface. It may be calculated or it may be measured by filling the instrument with a Newtonian fluid whose viscosity has been accurately determined by another method. Once this relation has been determined, the factor by which the total torque must be reduced to give that arising solely from the flow in the annulus may be calculated and this factor thereafter always be used. In practice this factor is often taken into consideration in arriving at the instrument manufacturer's calibration. This factor, however, applies only when the sample is Newtonian and when the viscometer is always reassembled in exactly the same position. If the distance between the bases is not held constant, or if the cylinder is not covered to exactly the same depth, the factor will be wrong and an unknown error will be introduced into the results. When the sample is non-Newtonian a different situation arises. Considering only zone B, the shear rate in this zone varies from zero at the axis to a maximum value which depends on the separation of the plates. The fraction of the total torque contributed by this zone will now depend upon the properties of the sample and cannot be eliminated by applying the (Newtonian) constant factor.

By way of an example, consider a viscometer in which the cylinders have radii 22·5 and 25 mm; the inner cylinder is 50 mm long and its base is 10 mm above the outer. With a Newtonian fluid the torque on the base is 3·67% of that on the cylindrical surface. When the viscometer is filled with a power law fluid whose exponent α is 0·7, this figure is increased to 5·92%. A calibration of the stress, correctly allowing for the torque on the base when the fluid is Newtonian, would now be in error by more than 2%. When the exponent is 0·3 the base zone would account for over 10% of the total torque and nearly 14% when the exponent is 0·1.

The effect of this on the accuracy of a flow curve may be seen if this viscometer is used for determining the flow curve of a material with a yield value. Suppose that the true flow curve is generally of the same shape as that given by the Casson equation (Fig. 13). At high values of shear rate $d\ln\tau/d\ln\dot{\gamma}$ is near unity and calibration of the viscometer with a Newtonian fluid is near enough accurate. As the shear rate is decreased, the slope of the curve becomes less. At first the shear rate calibration is not seriously affected, but the shear stress becomes progressively less than that indicated until the error is about 5% when $d\ln\tau/d\ln\dot{\gamma}$ is 0·5. As the shear rate decreases further, both the indicated shear rate and stress increase in error. At $d\ln\tau/d\ln\dot{\gamma} = 0\cdot1$ both are in error by more than 10%, and as the curve flattens out towards the yield stress the shear rate error increases more rapidly than the stress error. The whole shape of the curve is distorted and the yield stress measured is incorrect. If the effect of the zone above the inner cylinder is also considered, these errors are all increased.

Sometimes the ends of the cylinders are conical instead of flat. If the apex of the cone just touches the base of the outer cylinder, this ensures a constant shear rate in zone B, though this is unlikely to be equal to the effective shear rate in zone A. In the example just quoted, the angle between the cone and the base would have to be 6° and the cone would have to be positioned accurately to within a few microns. Even so, the relative contributions to the torque from the two zones would not be constant: the exponent appears in different form in the two expressions. More usually the cone angle is greater than this and the apex does not touch the bottom. The result is not so much to improve the accuracy of calibration as to ease filling the viscometer and to improve the stability at high flow rates.

Two other devices may be adopted which mitigate the 'end effect'. If the viscometer is provided with an efficient guard ring, so that zones B and C are effectively excluded, only the torque transmitted across zone A will be measured. Manufacturers are loth to do this, as it adds considerably to the cost of the instrument and users find it tedious to handle. Nevertheless, if accuracy in the stress calibration is important, it is strongly recommended. A compromise is achieved in some viscometers. The lower face of the inner cylinder is hollowed out as in the dotted line in Fig. 22. If the viscometer is then filled carefully from below (i.e. into zone B), an air bell is trapped between the fluid and the base of the inner cylinder and this cylinder therefore rests on a cushion of air, which provides a low-friction bearing. If the upper surface is similarly hollowed out, any superfluous fluid overflows into this hollow and zone C disappears. The only torque not accounted for by the annulus is now that from the corner between zones A and B, and this is relatively small. Variations in this due to non-Newtonian properties of the sample cause a much smaller, and maybe acceptably small, error in calibration than when the surfaces are flat.

The cone and plate and the parallel plate instruments are virtually free from the potential sources of error which are inherent in the concentric cylinder viscometer. In these, provided that proper care has been taken to fill the sample space, this space completely defines the field in which the measured flow takes place. This is not quite true with the cone and plate: in any practical realization of this geometry, the apex of the cone is truncated so that there is no risk of an undefined friction between the cone and the plate at the point at which they would make contact. The result of this is that the central space, near the axis, is a small zone which is in effect a parallel plate viscometer. However, recalling that the total torque resulting from a stress applied over any area is proportional to the cube of the radius (eqn (67)), it can be seen that removing up to a tenth of the cone at its apex can introduce errors only of the order of 0·1% and this is for almost all purposes too small to be significant.

In compression-testing instruments, where only the sample length is defined by the instrument and the dimensions normal to this are free from any instrumental constraint, a somewhat different situation arises. Simple theory, as enunciated above, assumes that the sample is homogeneous and isotropic and that as its length changes under the action of a load, its cross-sectional area will change strictly in inverse proportion at all points along its length. That is, a cylindrical sample will remain a cylindrical sample, or a right prism will remain a similar right prism, though each will be elongated or foreshortened. As a consequence of this, a constant load is not to be equated to a constant stress, nor is a constant (linear) rate of compression to be equated to a constant strain rate. Instruments have been devised to compensate mechanically for changes in cross-section, but these have never found favour with manufacturers because they are usually clumsy and restrict the versatility of the instrument in other ways. It is perfectly feasible, however, to achieve electronic control, by means of a simple feedback system, and this is to be recommended should this refinement be desired.

Unfortunately the provision of a proportioning device to compensate for cross-sectional changes is likely to be misleading. It presupposes that the sample will retain its original shape. In practice there are two factors which must be taken into account. If there is any friction between the surface of the sample and the plates of the instrument, the flow of the sample in contact with the plates in any direction normal to the loading will be restricted and that portion of the sample will behave as if it had a yield value in that direction only. As a consequence the deformed sample becomes barrel-shaped, as in Fig. 23(a). If on the other hand the plates are

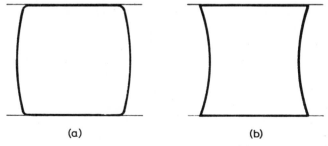

(a)   (b)

FIG. 23. Distortion of compressed cylindrical samples: (a) plates not lubricated, (b) plates lubricated.

perfectly smooth (or lubricated), this restraint is eliminated but the shape of the sample under stress now depends on the properties of the material. If it is a perfectly elastic Hookean solid, it will indeed retain its geometrical shape, taking up its new dimensions instantaneously upon the application of any load. However, if it is a viscoelastic material, which is more likely if it is of interest to the food rheologist, this will no longer apply. It will be remembered from the earlier discussion of viscoelastic behaviour that these materials do not take up their final equilibrium instantaneously, but that the attainment of that equilibrium is characterized by a time constant.

If we consider the behaviour of a thin slice of the material under the action of a compressive load, the mass balance requires that the displacement normal to the direction of compression is inversely proportional to the square root of the compression, and their derivatives—the velocities—bear the same relation. This is incompatible with the constitutive equation for a viscoelastic material if the stress is supposed to be distributed equally in all three mutually perpendicular directions. An infinitely thin layer at the contact surface between the sample and the plate of the instrument, if this is assumed to be perfectly lubricated, will not be subject to any viscous drag as it moves in a radial direction and the incompatibility disappears. The contiguous layers are, however, subject to viscous drag through the internal viscosity of the sample, and the isotropic nature of the characteristic time is preserved only if the distribution of the stress in the three directions is modified, with an increase in the axial direction and a decrease in the normal directions. The effect of this is cumulative as one moves away from the end plates and the result is that the sample deforms in the shape shown in Fig. 23(b). A mathematical expression of this and of its effect on the shape of the creep curve obtained with the instrument can be derived if a suitable model is assumed, and also if it is assumed that the sample is ideally homogeneous and isotropic. These conditions and the condition that the surface is perfectly lubricated are unlikely to be fulfilled in any practical application. As long as the total deformation is small, the effect of this distortion in shape is not likely to be significant, but if larger deformations are envisaged, then the distortion, whether it be of the form of Fig. 23(a) or (b), must be expected to reduce the accuracy attainable.

A further consequence of the effect of the characteristic time associated with the material is that the Deborah number may affect the measurement. If the compression is carried out at a constant rate, such that the characteristic time of the displacement is of a similar order of magnitude as the relaxation time of the sample material, then some stress relaxation may take place during the course of the measurement, and the force–

compression curve obtained is not a true representation of the properties of the material. It is possible to correct the curve in this case, either using a relaxation time determined independently or empirically from the curve itself. A correction is, however, satisfactory only if the material conforms to a known simple model.

Before leaving the subject of instrumental accuracy finally, it is worth considering what any claimed accuracy implies in the precision of the setting of the apparatus and the physical dimensions of the sample. Taking first the concentric cylinder viscometer given as an example in an earlier paragraph, and considering only the flow in the annular gap, an error in the radius of the inner cylinder of only $2 \cdot 39$ μm or in the outer cylinder of $2 \cdot 65$ μm would give rise to an error of $0 \cdot 1\%$ in the representative shear rate. It follows that, to be sure of an accuracy of $\pm 0 \cdot 1\%$, the radius of each cylinder must be known to within little more than ± 1 μm and that this must be maintained throughout the life of the instrument in spite of any wear and tear. As the ratio r_1/r_2 gets closer to unity, so the requirement becomes more stringent. In one commercial viscometer the tolerance on the radii is only $\pm 0 \cdot 25$ μm for a $0 \cdot 1\%$ accuracy.

In a parallel plate instrument there is only one dimension of any consequence. An effective shear rate has no significance with this configuration, but the calculated material parameter, be it a viscosity or a rigidity, varies with the separation of the plates. Simply, then, $\pm 0 \cdot 1\%$ accuracy in the material parameter requires a similar accuracy in the separation.

There are two factors of importance in the cone and plate geometry, the angle of the cone and the accuracy with which it can be set in relation to the plate. The shear in the sample space is directly proportional to the tangent of the semi-apical angle of the cone. If the angle between the cone and the plate is $1°$, which is fairly common in commercial instruments, this must be known to within $\pm 0 \cdot 001°$ if one wishes to achieve $0 \cdot 1\%$ accuracy. It is possible, but expensive, to manufacture cones with this degree of accuracy. It is more likely that any cone on a reasonably priced instrument is manufactured to be approximately correct; if a high accuracy is demanded, then the exact angle must be determined subsequently. It is probably wiser to do this indirectly by calibrating the instrument carefully with a liquid of known viscosity than to attempt the direct measurement of the angle, unless the facilities of a metrology laboratory are accessible. Even when the cone angle is known with sufficient accuracy, this is of no value unless the instrument can be set up correctly. From the basic equation for this viscometer, eqn (67), it can be deduced that when the separation of the plates is in error by only a small amount, h, say, the fractional error in the measurement is given by $3h \cot \varphi/2a$, to a close approximation. If the angle is 1°, as before, and the radius of the plate is 25 mm, to achieve an accuracy of $\pm 0\cdot 1\%$ the separation of the plates must be correct to within ± 582 nm. Since this is approximately the wavelength of light, a corollary of this is that the surfaces must be of near-optical quality.

The main problem with compression tests is in the cross-section of the sample. If the sample is large enough and the material firm, there is no difficulty in measuring its dimensions with more than adequate accuracy with a micrometer. But of course this is not always possible. If the sample is heterogeneous, such as bread crumb or compressed sausage meat, it may be somewhat irregular whatever care may have been taken in preparing it in the desired shape. Measurement of its dimensions becomes more tedious and less exact. It may well be necessary in these circumstances to accept that only limited accuracy can reasonably be achieved.

From what has been said in the preceding paragraphs, it will be obvious that $\pm 0\cdot 1\%$ is a very high standard of accuracy to attain. In very many circumstances it may be quite unjustifiable in both time and expense to take all the precautions necessary to achieve it. Then a lower order of accuracy may be quite acceptable. However, the philosophy remains the same, and the experimenter should always take the necessary and sufficient precautions to ensure that he achieves the accuracy that he desires. It is just that the tolerances will be that much greater than in the examples given. These remarks on accuracy have applied only to the measurements: it follows that any rheological parameters derived from them cannot be any more accurate than the measurements themselves, even if the correct rheological model be chosen to describe the behaviour. It cannot be too strongly stressed that the limitation in accuracy should always be borne in mind when quoting any rheological measurements. By the same token, it is quite in order to view published results with a healthy scepticism when the accuracy, either claimed or implied, appears to be unreasonable.

CHAPTER 7

Classification

In the early chapters some ideas were developed which showed how certain characteristic patterns of rheological behaviour could be expected to arise from the organization of the components making up a complex system such as a food substance. Following this, some models were described which have been found useful as a shorthand for simplifying a description of that behaviour. In the last few chapters some of the methods of making measurements of that behaviour have been described and, in particular, emphasis has been placed on the problems of disentangling the relevant information about the sample from the performance of the apparatus. It now remains to return to the question of structure and to see to what extent measurements which have actually been made have led to an insight into that structural organization. With this object in view, a few different materials have been selected. These have been chosen as representatives of different types of materials and because different methods of approach have been used. It is of some interest to notice here again the interaction between sample and model and instrumental measurement and to see how the choice of the combination of model and measurement has contributed to the interpretation. Sometimes the choice has been deliberate. But it is obvious to the student of the history of food rheology that different techniques have become associated with different products; often this has arisen by way of a historical accident, because a particular pioneer in his specialized field possessed a particular instrument. Fortunately nowadays there is more dialogue between rheologists in different branches of the food industry. It is hoped that the measure of success achieved by various approaches described in the ensuing pages may help in the cross-fertilization of ideas and encourage others to realize that several techniques may be equally viable and even complementary.

Whenever attempts are made to classify a number of different entities according to some preconceived idea, there inevitably remain a few left over which defy the system. The rheologist attempting to classify foodstuffs according to their characteristic behaviour encounters this problem sooner than most. Rheology has already been defined as a study of that grey area of materials which lie between liquid and solid, and who shall decide where one shade of grey passes to the next. Nevertheless, it is possible to divide most food materials encountered into a few main categories according to their rheological behaviour, even though the boundaries between them may remain blurred. As far as possible, examples have been taken from each main category, together with one— cheese—which transcends all the boundaries during the course of its development.

Perhaps the most easily recognizable group comprises the fluids. From the present point of view these are distinguished by the fact that their properties are usually studied by one or other viscometric method. Milk and cream and the fruit juices fall readily into this category. To these may be added raw egg, starch and protein suspensions and some protein dopes. Still in the realm of fluids come the pastes. These may be studied by viscometry or it may be more appropriate to use creep methods. They are usually recognized as materials with some sort of structure, often of an irregular nature, though their main unifying feature is that they contain discrete particulate matter in a continuous fluid phase. Butter, dough and sausage meat may be included in this group. In an extreme case, when the continuous phase is air, these are, of course, the powders. These, however, do not usually respond to conventional rheological techniques: their obvious lack of cohesion presents special problems and they require the application of special methods.

On the solid side, food materials may be divided into those which possess a highly organized structure and those whose structure is essentially of a random nature. In the first group the hydrocolloid gels are an outstanding example. The second group are the solid counterpart of the fluid suspensions, materials comprising discrete particles surrounded by a continuous solid rather than fluid phase. Chocolate below its melting point is a good example of this type of material. It is usually most appropriate to examine these solids by creep or relaxation methods or by small strain oscillatory tests.

There are still a few foods which remain untidily outside even this loose classification. Natural fruits and vegetables are 'solids' with well-organized structures, but these structures are often of a different order of complexity from other foods, which are usually prepared foods. For the purposes of academic study it may be of interest to apply conventional rheological methods to the examination of parts of a fruit or vegetable, such as for example the flesh of a potato, but the commonest interest in the whole viand is in its eating quality, a textural property and therefore strictly outside the scope of this work, but which may be indicated by use of one or more empirical tests. Another anomalous food is the boiled sweet. This, in spite of its appearance, is not a solid, but a suspension of other ingredients in a substrate of a sugar glass. Since glasses are strictly Newtonian fluids of high viscosity, boiled sweets should properly be classified among the fluids, but the order of magnitude of the viscosity is so far removed from that of other fluids that conventional fluid rheological methods are inappropriate.

CHAPTER 8

Measurements on Some Fluids and Their Interpretation

By definition fluids are materials which flow. Therefore it should be possible to measure their properties by any viscometric method. In practice there are several reservations to this general statement which must be made. The most reliable method will depend upon the properties of the fluid. All the fluids of interest to the food rheologist, with the exception of a few vegetable oils, are solutions of large molecules, or suspensions of particles, which may be liquid or solid and of colloidal dimensions or greater, or often more complex combinations of both. In view of what has been written earlier about the importance of the size factor in determining the reliability of measurements, it will be realized that the dimensions of the largest particles in a suspension will influence the suitability of any particular instrument. For example, if a cone and plate viscometer, or a parallel plate viscometer, is to be used, the distance between the plates must be sufficiently great for the sample between them to be properly representative. If, however, the sample is one of the less viscous fluids, it may well be that it is difficult to retain it within the sample space unless the gap between the plates is sufficiently small for the surface tension forces at the periphery to act as a retaining barrier. These requirements may be mutually exclusive.

Milk and its derivatives, condensed and evaporated milk and dairy cream, all contain globules whose diameter may be up to 10 μm; mayonnaise contains even larger globules, perhaps up to 30 μm or more in diameter; egg yolk contains granules of 30 μm diameter; honey contains particles of pollen; fruit juices and purees may contain quite large pieces of debris from the pulp up to 0·1 mm in the longest dimension. These are all rheological fluids. With milk and its derivatives, then, the size factor may be relatively unimportant, though even here the results with a cone and plate viscometer whose plates are separated in the axial regions by a distance not much greater than the largest globule must be treated cautiously. On the other hand, when the sample is a puree, the sample within such a viscometer may depart appreciably from being representative of the whole. The argument may be applied in a similar way to include capillary viscometers. The bore of any capillary should be large when compared with the largest suspended particle. Whilst almost any capillary viscometer may be suitable for the measurement of the viscosity of a solution of macromolecules, none may be of wide enough bore to be suitable for a puree. A general principle may thus be enunciated. The use of a small gap viscometer, of whatever geometry, cannot be recommended for heterogeneous fluid foods: any results obtained using one should be treated with some caution, the reliability decreasing as the size of the suspended particles increases. This is not to impugn the many measurements which have already been made by numerous research workers, but to draw attention to the fact that any interpretation of these measurements must be made with a degree of caution appropriate to the structure of the sample.

On the other hand, it may be considered expedient to use a concentric cylinder viscometer, because of its obvious advantages in retaining the sample and the ease with which it can be operated. Then, if the sample should prove to be a long way from Newtonian, the absolute accuracy may suffer in a way that was described in Chapter 6. Once more there is a dichotomy to be resolved. Inevitably there must be some compromise. This need not be very disturbing provided that the nature of the compromise and its implications are fully understood, both by the experimenter and by the reader of the published results. Many of the measurements which are referred to in the present chapter have been made using concentric cylinder viscometers. In some cases, absolute accuracy may have suffered: this must be borne in mind when any numerical values are quoted. On the other hand, because of the convenience in operating this viscometer, the instrumental precision may generally be expected to be of a high order, so that any comparisons within a single experiment should be very worth while.

If the sample is treated as a continuum, measurements of its rheological properties should not depend upon the method or type of instrument used and numerical values of the appropriate parameters may be calculated, using the theory outlined in the earlier chapters, which will uniquely specify those properties. However, it will be found that, when the sample is a composite material, the rheological properties are influenced both by any interactions between its structural components and also by the very fact that it is a composite. Different methods of measurement may well give rise to apparently conflicting results. It is necessary to consider how an understanding of the composite nature of the material may enable one to resolve this conflict. Milk and cream are a useful example to take as they have been extensively studied and are well documented. In the following paragraphs the discussion is based mainly on measurements on cream, but the lines of thought underlying the argument may equally be applied to any composite fluid.

Let us first consider the measurements made using a viscometer in oscillatory motion. It is often recommended that oscillatory measurements should be made at low amplitudes of shear in order to avoid unduly disturbing any structure in the sample material. This advice may be valid when the material possesses a delicate structure such as may occur, for example, in a weak gel. When the material is a composite fluid which has no organized structure an entirely different set of circumstances obtains and the parity between direct motion and oscillatory measurements may disappear. The response to an oscillatory motion is now very dependent upon the amplitude of the oscillation. This may be demonstrated by means of the torsion pendulum viscometer. Although this instrument does not permit of precise measurements of any useful rheological parameters when the sample fluid is cream, it does cover a wide spectrum of shear amplitudes in a single experiment. If the free member of the viscometer is originally displaced through a large enough angle so that the total shear amplitude during the first free swing is, say, several units, the amplitude during the first few oscillations decreases in the manner that would be expected for a pseudoplastic sample, i.e. the decrement increases with each swing. However, as the amplitude becomes small, the decrement begins to decrease quite markedly and the period of the oscillation increases slightly as if the sample is now slightly elastic. It is possible to calculate a 'mean viscosity' for each swing and if this is plotted against the mean shear rate during the course of that swing, a curve such as Fig. 24 is obtained. It must be remembered when reading this graph that the course of the experiment is from right to left. For the purpose of comparison the flow curve for the same sample as determined by a direct rotation experiment is shown on the same figure as a broken line. The most interesting feature is that at low shear particularly the torsion pendulum curve resembles the transient response which occurs as shear increases at the onset of rotation in the continuous rotation viscometer (cf. Fig. 10).

If the experiment is carried out in the more conventional manner, with a fixed amplitude, well below unit shear, and fixed period and the stress plotted against the strain, an open loop is obtained. Provided that the oscillation is slow enough compared with the time of response of the measuring system, it will be seen that the loop is not an ellipse, but is rather like a parallelogram with the corners rounded. Figure 25 shows one such loop for which the period was 10 s. The most important feature of this curve is the very rapid decay of stress in the neighbourhood of the extreme excursion of the moving plate, which is when the plate is more or less at

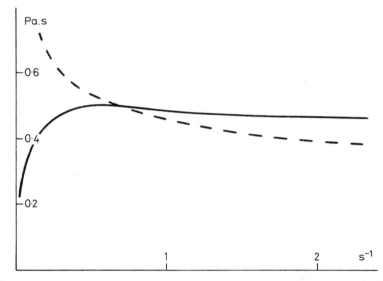

FIG. 24. Apparent flow curves for a cream: ——, as determined by a torsion pendulum viscometer; ---, as determined by a rotation viscometer.

rest. This gives the key to the interpretation of the loop. If we recall the description given of the behaviour of a suspension in flow (pp. 30–2), it will be remembered that when the flow ceases the particles which have been disturbed fall back rapidly into their original (uncrowded) state. We may then begin to follow the cycle through, starting at a rest position. Although this is conventionally a position of maximum strain, in this case, by virtue of the collapse of the enforced organization of the suspended particles, that strain has been dissipated and to all intents and purposes a new programme of flow is commencing. As the strain increases, so does the resistance to flow because of the displacement of the particles from their random equi-

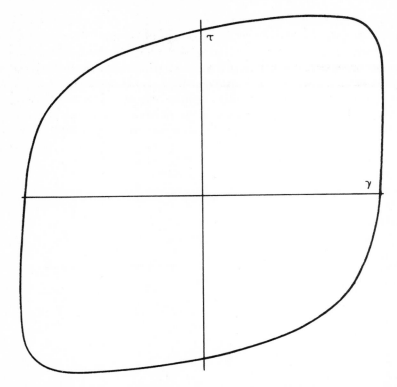

F𝙸𝙶. 25. Stress–strain loop obtained with a cream sample in an oscillating viscometer.

librium positions. This reorganization continues past the point at which the rate of strain is maximum, until an equilibrium condition is reached where the rate of reorganization of the particles due to the imposed shear is matched by the rate at which they tend to return to their random positions. At this moment, in Fig. 25 about 1·2 s before the end of the half-cycle, the stress required to sustain the motion is a maximum. Thereafter it falls as the rate of shearing is no longer adequate to maintain as much reorganization, until at the end of the first half-cycle, when motion ceases, the structure collapses completely and the second half-cycle repeats the pattern in the reverse direction. In this example the stress actually reached zero about one-third of a second after the end of the forward motion. This is due to the fact that a finite time is required for the complete reestablishment of the original structure. It may be deduced that this lapse of time gives a rough estimate of the characteristic time associated with this recovery. This characteristic time will of course also influence the point at which the stress no longer rises. If the rate of oscillation is increased, the time lapse between cessation of forward motion (in either direction) and the fall to zero stress will be a larger fraction of the cycle, so that the shape of the curve will approximate more closely to an ellipse and eventually the cream will appear to be viscoelastic. If the dynamic measurements are analysed as if the sample were truly viscoelastic, it is this apparent elasticity which will be obtained for the elastic component, whilst the viscous component will be some figure which corresponds to the resistance to the flow averaged over the cycle. It will not necessarily bear any relation to the viscosity measured in equilibrium conditions at any particular shear rate.

It is of some interest in this connection to consider the performance of the forced resonance type of viscometer. A sample of cream in this viscometer gives a response curve such as Fig. 26. This is clearly not unlike

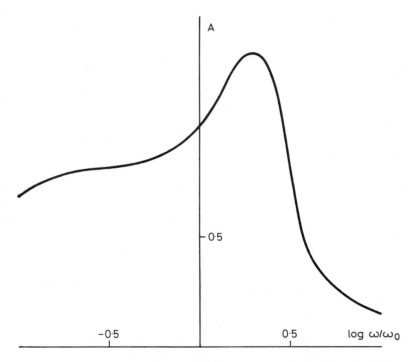

FIG. 26. Response of a forced resonance viscometer containing a sample of cream.

the response expected for a viscoelastic material, except that at low frequencies (and hence low rates of shear) the response falls away more like that of a Newtonian fluid. It is this tail at the low-frequency end which is characteristic of the suspension and serves to distinguish it from a material which has a real elasticity. At the low-frequency end the rate at which the sample is deformed is so slow that the suspended particles fall back into their rest array almost as rapidly as they are displaced and the sample has an Einstein-type viscosity. In the immediate vicinity of the true resonance frequency, the shear and the shear rate are very small and there is a slight tendency for a shoulder to appear on the curve, but on the high-frequency side particularly, the apparent elasticity quickly becomes evident and the shape of the curve is very reminiscent of that for a Kelvin body (Fig. 16). There is no point in attempting to calculate any parameters from this curve since it does not correspond to any specific model. It serves only to differentiate the behaviour of the sample from that of either a Newtonian fluid or a viscoelastic material.

Finally we may consider what happens when the cream is studied by a creep method. It has been reported that, on the application of the stress, there is an instantaneous compliance which, since it is instantaneous, is assumed to be elastic in origin. However, this is an imprecise statement. What is meant is that there is a compliance which is so rapid that its time constant is less than the time constant of the measuring system. Thereafter the strain continues to increase, though at a reducing rate. This is as may be predicted from the structure of the cream. On the application of the stress the first effect is for the layers in contact with the walls of the apparatus to be sheared. This will take place rapidly at a speed determined by the viscosity of the serum, as the suspension is depleted in this region. When these layers have taken up the stress, the bulk of the sample will then be sheared and the suspended particles in the random array gradually displaced. At first the flow will be that given by the Einstein-type theory, but as the particles are displaced from their natural equilibrium positions the resistance will continue to rise. The creep curve will be the exact transform of the early stages of the transient flow curve. On removal of the stress the flow ceases abruptly and the original array reestablishes itself without doing any external work—there is no elastic recoil.

We have now seen that, when the rheological properties of cream are measured by different methods, disparate numerical values for the viscous and elastic components are obtained if the sample is assumed to behave as a continuum. However, by taking into consideration the fact that it is a concentrated suspension of particles in a random array without any organized structure, as was described on p. 31, all the differences may be explained. If we take this argument in reverse, we can propose a general maxim that when an unknown sample has different patterns of behaviour when subject to different methods of testing, the possibility of a discontinuous structure should be explored. This also leads to the conclusion that, if one is interested in the structure of the material, it is insufficient to confine one's measurements to one particular method; as many different rheological tests as possible should be brought to bear on the problem. Then, and only then, can a suitable model for the structure be proposed. No model may be considered entirely satisfactory unless it enables every facet of the rheological behaviour of the material to be predicted.

We have now seen how the composite nature of a fluid food may provide a framework for explaining, qualitatively at least, the general rheological behaviour. We can now proceed to consider how the composition and structure may influence some of the finer detail of that behaviour. For this purpose we will stay with the example of milk and cream. In the process of separation of cream from milk, if it is performed by a separator as in modern commercial practice, a very small amount of protein may be lost from the serum and there may be a small redistribution of protein and calcium salts between the surface of the fat globules and the colloidal substrate, but these changes are small enough to have no appreciable effect on the viscosity. Cream may, therefore, be regarded rheologically as milk with an enhanced content of fat globules, and milk and cream may be regarded as one species.

One characteristic which appears to be common to the vast majority of fluid foods is that their viscosity decreases with increasing shear rate: they are pseudoplastic. It has already been shown that when a sample is a simple two-phase system consisting of particulate matter suspended in a Newtonian fluid, hydrodynamic considerations alone are sufficient to account for this behaviour, provided that the concentration of the dispersed phase is high enough for steric rearrangements to result from the flow. However, non-Newtonian behaviour is often observed at much lower concentrations than would be expected on such a simple approach. The explanation must be sought in the interaction of all the components.

When milk is examined by means of a microscope, it appears as a suspension of fat globules in a slightly luminescent substrate. The globules are distributed spatially at random throughout the milk; there is no organized structure, though some of the globules may have joined to form doublets or higher aggregates. A random distribution of spherical globules with a concentration of some 3–4% might be expected to conform more or less to Einstein's law and should be Newtonian. In fact the agreement is not so good and significant departure from Newtonian behaviour has been observed in milk at room temperature, but not when heated above 40 °C. In order to find a satisfactory explanation it is better to build up a picture of the milk structure starting with the smallest ingredients.

The purely aqueous phase, or milk serum, is a dilute solution of mineral salts and lactose, together with some water-soluble proteins, principally lactalbumin and β-lactoglobulin. The sugar is present in a concentration of about 4% by weight. Allowing for the fact that in solution each sugar molecule is surrounded by a solvation shell, the volume concentration is still only between 2 and 3%. Adding to this the small contribution from the mineral salts and the soluble proteins, the serum may be expected to have a viscosity not more than 1·1 times that of pure water. The β-lactoglobulin is, as its name implies, a molecule which is more or less spherical in shape; only the lactalbumin is elongated and this is present in such small quantity that any tendency it may have to impart non-Newtonian behaviour to the serum is too small to be observable and may be discounted.

Suspended in this Newtonian serum is the principal protein, casein. This again, in natural milk, is roughly spherical and exists as both small individual units about 20 nm in cross-section and larger aggregates with a range of diameters up to and occasionally exceeding 200 nm. These aggregates, known as micelles, though unlike the micelles encountered with surfactants, are roughly spherical in shape and are loosely packed, having a porous texture somewhat like a sponge. Each micelle may entrap a considerable amount of the serum within its interstices. There is a lack of agreement between different experimenters about the correct allowance to be made for the amount of serum entrapped and the size of any solvation shell around the micelles. This lack of agreement may well arise from the fact that the measurements were carried out on milks of different origin. There is no exact distribution of the sizes of the casein aggregates which will apply equally to all milks; there are certainly variations of genetic origin and probably some due to different husbandry. Whilst individual casein units will not entrap any serum, having no interstices, but may have a solvation shell around them, large aggregates will entrap more or less constant proportions of serum, but possess a solvation shell related to their surface area. Clearly the balance between individual units, small aggregates and large aggregates will affect the average amount entrapped and hence the average specific volume. Notwithstanding this lack of agreement, the effective volume swept out by the micelles in rotation may be taken as somewhere between two and four times that which might be inferred from the weight and density of the casein alone.

Finally, suspended in this casein suspension are the fat globules. These are present in a distribution of sizes which is approximately log-normal centred around a mean diameter of about 3 μm, together with a somewhat variable excess of smaller droplets. Again the actual value is subject to some variation which has its origin in the genetics and husbandry of the cows. The net result of all the ingredients is that the whole milk comprises around 15% by volume of solids dispersed, either in solution or in suspension, in water. These solids have a wide distribution of sizes from small molecular dimensions up to around 10 μm for the fat globules, and very nearly all the particles are more or less spherical. This concentration is much too high for the Einstein equation to apply, but if Brinkman's modification is used, making plausible estimates for the size of the solvation shells and entrapped water, the concentration dependence of the viscosity of milk and cream, up to the concentration at which appreciable departure from Newtonian behaviour may be observed, is more or less correctly predicted.

So far the constitution of milk has been used to explain its viscosity, but no suggestions have been made which might account for the fact that it displays any pseudoplastic characteristics. Yet the viscosity of ordinary raw milk does show a shear rate dependence at temperatures below about 40 °C. It is also known that the viscosity of cream is highly dependent on the temperature treatment during processing. The viscosity predicted by the methods of the preceding paragraph is that measured at high shear rates and for cream which has been separated at temperatures well above 40 °C. In order to find an explanation of the non-Newtonian effects, we may look at some early work carried out nearly a hundred years ago on the effect of the temperature to which milk was heated before separation on the properties of the cream. Cream separated at low temperature was observed to be more viscous than that separated at high. This was attributed at that time to a substance called 'agglutinin'. At temperatures below about 40 °C this was believed to be adsorbed on the surface of the fat globules and when it bridged two globules it acted as a cement binding them together. At higher temperatures the agglutinin was said to migrate into the substrate from the globule surface so that the globules became perfectly discrete. The behaviour of 'agglutinin' is now known to be a characteristic of the immunoglobulins. Since only one molecule of immunoglobulin is required to bind two fat globules, the presence of a very small quantity of immunoglobulin is sufficient to cause some considerable clustering of the fat globules in the milk.

We can now propose the following hypothesis for the rheological behaviour of milk. The fundamental viscosity, which is that measured at high shear rates or at temperatures above 40 °C, is accounted for by the presence of all the components considered together. In this condition, each fat globule and indeed every other particle in suspension is considered to be discrete. However, below 40 °C, in the rest condition, some of the globules may be joined to others by immunoglobulin bridges. A certain amount of extra work is required to rotate the resulting clusters and ultimately to break the bridges. This appears as an enhanced viscosity. As the shear rate increases, the rate of doing work increases and the proportional excess viscosity diminishes until at a sufficiently high shear rate, for which a figure of the order of 300 s^{-1} has been quoted, the particles are all discrete and the milk becomes Newtonian. Above 40 °C the bridges disappear because the immunoglobulins have lost their affinity for the fat globules and the milk is Newtonian at all shear rates.

If the above argument is extended to practical dairying operations, it becomes evident that, in order to produce a cream which has a high viscosity in relation to its fat content, the operations should be carried out so that the conditions are favourable for the maximum clustering of the globules. Most important is the temperature during separation. This should be held well below 40 °C. Subsequent processing may modify the properties of the cream further, but unless the capacity to build bridges between the globules is retained in the cream at this stage, no amount of further processing can replace it. Figure 27 shows some results from experiments designed to show the variation of the properties of cream with the concentration of the fat. The creams were all produced from the same supply of milk and in the same plant. The apparent viscosity at unit shear rate for each cream in this example has been obtained from the experimental data by interpolation using the best-fitting power law. The solid line shows the variation of viscosity with fat concentration for those creams which were separated at temperatures of 43 and 49 °C. The results for these two temperatures were combined because there was no significant difference between them. On the other hand, the viscosity of cream at any concentration when separated at 37 °C, indicated by the broken line, was always appreciably higher.

In the laboratory it is possible to carry out an experiment, somewhat reminiscent of a genetic breeding experiment, which provides further corroboration of the effect of temperature. If a single supply of milk is divided into two portions, one portion separated into cream and skim milk at a low temperature (say 35 °C) and the other at a high temperature (say 45 °C), then, according to the above hypothesis, the immunoglobulins in the first should be concentrated in the cream, whilst in the second they should be concentrated in the skim milk. The first cream is, as expected, more viscous than the second. If now the cream separated at the lower temperature is mixed with the skim milk separated at the higher temperature, the resulting reconstituted milk should be identical in composition with the original apart from having an enhanced immunoglobulin content. If milk is reconstituted from the remaining portions, this should be deficient in immunoglobulin. The reconstituted milks can now be divided again and separated at low and high temperatures. In the cream which has been twice

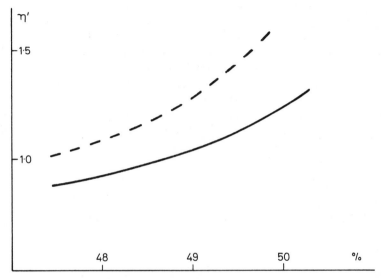

FIG. 27. Effect of sample preparation on apparent viscosity: ——, creams separated at a temperature above 40 °C; ———, creams separated below 40 °C.

separated at the low temperature, the conditions should be doubly favourable for clustering of the globules and a particularly thick cream result. All the others should be deficient in clustering ability and so thinner than normal. This experiment was first carried out many years ago when the cream was separated in pans under the action of gravity, and it was this result that led to the 'agglutinin' theory. It has been repeated more recently, using modern centrifugal separators. In fact the cream produced in the latter case by twice separating at low temperature was very viscous indeed and its viscosity was found to be highly dependent on shear rate.

It is a corollary of this hypothesis that, since the same agent is responsible for both the enhancement of the viscosity and for the amount by which it may be broken down through shearing, they should not be independent of each other. It has been shown that the flow curve for ordinary dairy cream may be described with fair accuracy over several decades of shear rate by a power law. The rheological properties may therefore be described by two parameters, the apparent viscosity at unit shear rate (the consistency index) and the exponent of the shear rate. In Fig. 28 some measured values of the two parameters have been plotted. These have been taken from some experiments carried out on consecutive production runs from a single commercial plant. All the samples had nominally the same fat content, 48%. It is not unreasonable to suppose that within the space of a few days, the bulk supply of the original milk would not have varied appreciably, so that the relative proportions of the major constituents and their size and size distributions would have remained substantially constant. It may be seen that there was clear evidence of an interdependence of the two parameters as suggested above. On the other hand, if creams are selected at random from many sources, no such clear relation exists, though there is still a tendency for the more viscous creams to be more pseudoplastic.

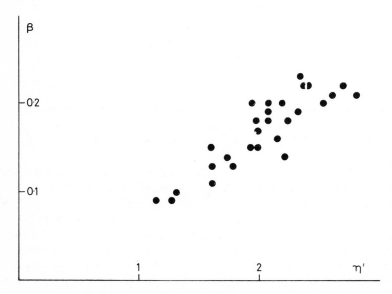

Fig. 28. Interrelation of power law parameters for cream samples from a single source.

The hypothesis as presented above is probably unduly naïve. Many experimenters have observed that greater clustering of the fat globules and an enhanced viscosity occur when 'free fat' is present. This is fat which is not in globules completely surrounded and isolated from the serum by a sheath or membrane. However, it is difficult to see how this free fat could, by itself, act as a bridge between contiguous intact globules, because these are surrounded by an entire sheath which presents a hydrophilic surface to the outside, the surface having an affinity for fat facing inwards towards the globule. Some cementing agent must be necessary. It is possible that casein provides this cement and some of the casein and the free fat combine to form bridges. It would be helpful in providing corroboration of these ideas if it were possible to see the globule clusters in detail. In order to obtain a clear microscope image, cream must be diluted several hundredfold and even then the globules are so small that no detail can be seen on their surfaces. In order to resolve fine details it is necessary to use an electron microscope: the dehydration of the sample which is necessary in preparing a specimen for electron microscopy may well involve the risk of destroying the very structure which it is wished to observe. For the present, then, we must rely on inference.

The point which arises from this example, and which cannot be too highly stressed, is that a knowledge of the role of the principal constituents may not be sufficient. The gross structure of a material may provide a framework for the basic rheological behaviour, but in the end it may well be that the most important contribution to, or the explanation of, any peculiarity may be the presence of a relatively minor constituent. In this case a constituent whose presence is measured in parts per million is suggested as contributing more to the non-Newtonian characteristics than all those which form the bulk of the material. The food rheologist may well find that it is more profitable to spend time studying the effect of a minor constituent than to study the gross structure, once he has identified the right constituent to study.

When milk is homogenized, a different state of affairs results. Although the primary reason for homogenization is to reduce the size of the fat globules, destroying the log-normal distribution and replacing it with one which is more nearly Gaussian, centred around a smaller size, in fact this is not the only change that takes place. In the first place there is a consider-able fragmention of the globules, so that the number of very small ones increases and the size is not truly homogeneous. Moreover, since the diameter of the globules has been reduced, the total surface area has increased. For example, a reduction in diameter by a factor of 5 would be accompanied by a 5-fold increase in the total surface area. Now the existing 'membrane' cannot stretch and globules with free surfaces would be unstable, so the newly formed surface area must be covered with other material adsorbed from the substrate. In fact, electron micrographs show that the globules of homogenized milk are mainly covered with casein subunits. On the other hand the quantity of globulins present has not altered, so that the fraction of globules which can be cemented by them is drastically reduced. One would therefore expect the homogenized milk to depart from Newtonian behaviour less than the original. Such, indeed, is the case, whilst the viscosity is not substantially altered. However, because of the vastly greater number of fat globules, the distances separating them are considerably reduced. As the concentration is increased, this separating distance soon approaches the diameter of the casein micelles, so that steric hindrance between casein and globule becomes important, whereas it was minimal in ordinary cream until the fat concentration became high. If the mean diameter of the fat globules is 0·5 μm, the mean separation distance becomes commensurate with the size of the largest casein micelles when the concentration is only around 20%. For this reason alone then, the viscosity of homogenized cream may therefore be expected to increase more rapidly with fat concentration than the original before homogenization. Whilst the viscosity of homogenized milk is comparable with that of the original, the viscosity of high-fat cream may be increased by an order of magnitude by homogenization. This is in advance of any processing treatment which may be employed in the dairy industry to enhance further the body of the cream.

When milk is concentrated by evaporation, ultrafiltration or reverse osmosis, greater changes in its composition take place than in cream production. In evaporation, only water is removed, so that the serum becomes more concentrated; in the other two processes some of the soluble constituents are also lost. In every case there result concentration changes such that the balance between the ionic components and the protein is upset. This has a destabilizing influence on the casein micelles and they tend to lose their globular shape. As might be expected, this leads to an enhanced viscosity and a greater shear-thinning behaviour. The viscosity rises much more steeply with increasing concentration than it does in the case of cream. Measurements of the viscosity made on some skim milk concentrated by ultrafiltration and extrapolated, suggested that flow should virtually cease when the total solid content reached some 34%, that is, an approximately 4-fold concentration. This would impose an upper limit on the extent to which concentration could be carried out effectively by this process. However, higher concentrations have been obtained under laboratory conditions. It may be that the extrapolation is not justifiable as the flow pattern changes from that of a fluid to that of a slurry-like material.

The concentration of milk by evaporation or the manufacture of condensed milk introduces further complexities. In the first place, it is usually considered necessary to homogenize the milk before processing in order to give the emulsion sufficient stability in the plant. The salt balance may be modified by the addition of small quantities of salts, such as citrates, which occur naturally in the milk, according to the individual manufacturer's practice and national legal constraints. As the milk is heated, some denaturation of both the colloidal and water-soluble protein takes place. Some aggregation of the casein takes place, but this is not extensive—a figure of 50% has been quoted for the average increase in particle weight. Most of the interesting rheological developments take place after production has been completed. The most remarkable feature of these is the long time constant of these changes. This is of some concern to the manufacturers, since it governs the useful shelf life of their products. This is clearly not a diffusion process. Although the mean free path of any particle in the product is necessarily small because of the close packing, movement is not so restricted that it would account for changes on a time-scale of weeks or even months. What appears to happen is that slow changes in the protein take place, whereby it gradually unfolds somewhat and complexes of fat and protein appear, whilst the soluble whey proteins form a net-like structure which tends to enmesh the casein. The end product of the reactions is for the net-like structure to pervade the whole milk, giving rise eventually to gelation.

Fruit juices and purees together make up a rather different class of fluid foods. Unlike milk, which contains almost a complete spectrum of particle types and sizes up to microscopic size, the vast majority of which are spherical or nearly so, the fruit juices are more nearly simple two-phase systems. The substrate, irrespective of the origin of the juice, is an aqueous solution of mineral salts, natural sugars and pectin, together with specific organic acid radicles which provide the characteristic flavour. Floating in this serum is the particulate matter, which is primarily the cell wall debris from the fruit. This is largely fibrous, extended and flexible and may reach dimensions such that individual particles are visible to the naked eye, i.e. more than 100 μm. It will be evident that the size factor may become important when the properties of these juices and purees are measured. Another problem, too, may arise. The natural juices, particularly, are often not stable and some of the particulate matter may separate out, either floating to the surface or falling to the bottom, according to the density relative to that of the substrate. This tendency to separation may also occur under the action of centrifugal forces when the viscosity is being measured in a rotation viscometer, giving rise to a concentration gradient across the sample. This may be quite serious when high rates of rotation are required to achieve high shear rates. If this happens, it may outweigh any advantage in using a rotation viscometer. It has been suggested that the use of a capillary viscometer may then be a satisfactory compromise.

Orange juice may be considered to be a typical example of a fruit juice. The properties of the serum are a consequence of the concentration of sugars and pectin. Pectin is an extended molecule which polymerizes to form parallel arrays of fibrils whose mean length is on average some 25 times their width. With such a polymer in solution, basic theory suggests that pectin solutions should be shear-thinning at almost any concentration. This has been found to be true. Applying the same type of argument as was used to synthesize the behaviour of milk, the presence of sugars, sucrose or fructose, in the serum serves only to reduce the free volume in which the pectin fibrils may rotate. A solution of pectin and sugar is therefore more viscous and departs more from Newtonian behaviour than the pectin alone. Besides the purely hydrodynamic considerations, pectin polymers in the presence of sugar and acid have a tendency to join up in a weak three-dimensional network. This gives, in addition to the non-Newtonian behaviour, a yield value to the substrate.

Four different types of particles have been observed to float in this substrate. Three of them are fine particles, one needle-like with lengths up to about 3 μm, one globular with diameters around 0·5 μm and the third slightly larger and irregular. Besides these there are large particles extending up to 0·1 mm in length. These are the flexible particles derived from the fruit pulp. They vary considerably both in flexibility and in the roughness of their surface. When present in sufficient quantity these suspended particles act to reinforce the pectin network, but at low concentrations the effect is the opposite—the suspended particles tend to interfere with the formation of the network.

The final result is that the juice is a shear-thinning fluid with a yield stress. It is sometimes said that it is thixotropic, but it is not all true thixotropy. As the juice is sheared, the viscosity certainly decreases, but this is in part due to the fact that the coarse particles are fragile and some of them, which have been described as irregular rag-like bodies, break up into smaller fragments which are more symmetrical in shape. These do not reunite as the shear ceases, and the viscosity remains permanently lower after shearing. (The term 'rheomalaxis' was coined to describe this type of behaviour, but it has never found favour.)

At this point we may ask the questions: how real is the yield stress in any fruit juice? and how important is it that it should be a true yield stress? The first can be answered by performing a creep type of experiment, which can be carried out in a viscometer where the stress is applied as the independent variable. On the application of a very small stress, if there be a structure of any kind within the juice, some motion will ensue at first as the structure is distorted. The subsequent behaviour will indicate whether the sample really possesses a yield value. If, after the initial motion, the sample eventually comes to rest, supporting the stress which has been applied, then it can be affirmed that it possesses a yield value in excess of that stress. Proceeding in this way with ever-increasing stress, a point may be reached at which the creep pattern changes from one which asymptotically reaches a static equilibrium to one in which permanent motion is established. The stress at which this occurs is the yield stress of the sample. However, it may be that even with the smallest stress which it is possible to apply, a state of equilibrium may not be established. It could be argued that the sample may still have a yield value but that it is so small that it has already been exceeded. In this event a relaxation experiment will distinguish whether a true yield point exists. If, after the sample has been sheared, the motion is arrested, the stress would fall to zero instantaneously if the sample were a true liquid. When the sample has some structure the stress may decay more slowly. If there is indeed a yield stress, then that is the residual value to which the stress will decay and the absence of a yield stress will be indicated by the fact that the stress ultimately falls to zero. It must always be borne in mind, though, that relaxation is an asymptotic process and theoretically always takes infinite time to reach equilibrium. Hence the initial decay may appear to be quite rapid, but a long wait and considerable patience may be necessary before it can be finally decided whether or not there is any residual stress.

More usually in practice, a yield stress will have been determined by extrapolating a flow curve back to zero shear rate, using either a graphical method and a visual estimate of the shape of the curve to be continued, or some assumed mathematical model. In this case an 'apparent' yield stress will be obtained. It is often an act of faith that this is taken to be a true yield value. If the purpose of quoting a yield stress is for it to be used in conjunction with other parameters to enable a flow curve to be reconstructed, then whether it is real or apparent is quite irrelevant. On the other hand, one practical importance of a yield value in a juice is that it prevents particulate matter from separating from the serum. Since these particles are principally derived from the pulp of the fruit and are usually extensively hydrated, their specific gravity is not very different from that of the serum. Only a small yield stress is required in the serum to inhibit this separation. A simple calculation may be made. The net downward force on a spherical particle 0·1 mm in radius, whose specific gravity is 1·1, when immersed in water is only 4·1 nN. A yield stress of 0·13 Pa is sufficient to inhibit any tendency for this particle to settle out. On the other hand, were there to be no yield stress, this particle would fall at a rate of about 0·2 mm s^{-1}. In an ordinary fruit squash bottle it would reach the bottom in well under an hour. We may conclude that a yield stress of the order of a pascal may be quite sufficient to prevent any but the largest particles from separating out, but that it must be a true yield stress.

Other fruit juices have very similar patterns of behaviour to orange. The principal differences arise from differences of pectin content and in the nature of the debris from the pulp of the fruit. All have in common the fact that, when treated with pectolytic enzymes to destroy the pectin completely, the non-Newtonian behaviour disappears, the suspended solids being present in too small a concentration to give rise to a measurable departure from Newtonian, and the viscosity is reduced to near that of an aqueous solution of sucrose of the same concentration as the sugar in the juice. The same is not true of purees and some manufactured products such as tomato ketchup. There, the solid content is considerably greater and makes a significant contribution to the overall rheological properties. In tomato ketchup, unless the native enzymes have been destroyed during processing, these attack the biopolymeric material binding the cell walls, freeing cellulose in the form of fibres which then become entangled giving an adventitious random network structure to the material. The addition of acid, such as vinegar, in the course of the processing attacks the cell walls further. The result is an eventual build-up of viscosity which may be several times that of the product at the moment of being formed.

Measurements which have been made by several experimenters on fruit juices have usually led them to conclude that the non-Newtonian behaviour could be expressed adequately in terms of one or other form of a power law. Usually this has taken the form of the Herschel and Bulkeley equation. This, however, is not a very convenient equation to apply as there is no simple analytical method of estimating the yield stress from the raw data. Moreover, it has already been pointed out that the power law should be treated only as phenomenological description of rheological behaviour and used for interpolation within the range of the measurements. Some workers in this field have taken the power law further. If Casson's arguments are applied to a material whose substrate is already a power law fluid, one can deduce an expression

$$\tau^m = \tau_0^m + (\dot{\gamma}\eta)^m \tag{92}$$

where m is no longer ½ but is still fractional. It would be stretching credibility too far to believe that this equation had any theoretical background: Casson's arguments are not universally accepted and the power law is certainly not beyond challenge. Nevertheless this equation may be encountered as a convenient way of approximating to the flow curve using only three parameters.

For our purpose any form of power law is an unfortunate choice. It fails completely to give any estimate of the limiting viscosities at low and high shear rates which one might expect to be able to relate to the constitution of the purees. It is only possible to make some general observations on the basis of the power law. The presence of pulp increases the viscosity at all shear rates, as would be expected, and also gives rise to a greater departure from Newtonian behaviour. It appears in this respect to overshadow almost completely any departure from Newtonian behaviour due to the presence of pectin in the serum. Some experiments on tomato puree showed that, whilst the power law exponent α for the serum decreased from 0·95 to 0·67 as the solid matter in the puree increased from 6% to 30%, the exponent for the whole puree remained nearly constant around 0·45.

This constancy of exponent has been observed for samples of purees of other fruits. On the other hand, substantial differences occur between samples of the same species but of different origin. Knowledge of the composition of the puree does not appear to be sufficient to give an indication of its rheological properties. As far as can be ascertained, no studies have been reported in which measurements of rheological properties have been carried out in parallel with studies of the morphology of the puree. It would be interesting and instructive to see how, in particular, the limiting viscosities were influenced by the shape, size and concentration of the suspended particles.

The viscosity of most fruit juices and purees has been observed to vary less with temperature than that of the equivalent sugar solutions. This is to be expected in the case of purees, which contain a considerable amount of particulate matter, or juices whose pectin serum shows a yield stress. Only that part of the stress which contributes to the viscous flow is likely to be affected appreciably by the temperature. The rigidity of any network which may have built up in the material is, like any solid property, not very sensitive to temperature changes. So that part of the stress which is used up in overcoming the rigidity remains more or less constant.

In many cases other factors are much more predominant. Let us now return to the hydrodynamics of the flow. It will be recalled that the enhancement of the viscosity of a suspension of elongated particles over the value given by the Einstein-type theory has been attributed to the fact that some energy must be put into the system to cause the particles to rotate towards a direction in which their major axes lie along the direction of shear. At any stress there is a dynamic equilibrium when the applied stress is just balanced by the sum of that which is required to maintain the orientation of the particles against the forces tending to restore them to their natural random state and that which is required to maintain the flow with the particles in their new orientation. Only the second part is directly dependent on the viscosity of the substrate. When the particles are fully aligned along the direction of shear, the additional resistance to the flow arising from their presence is a minimum. With any other degree of

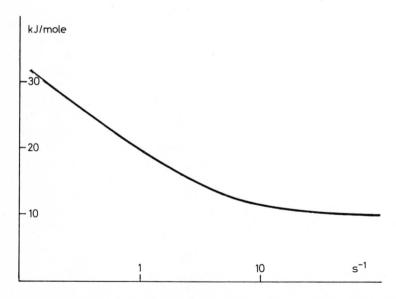

FIG. 29. Dependence of temperature coefficient of apparent viscosity on shear rate for an apple puree.

alignment the resistance is greater by a factor which depends on the shape of the particles and their inclination to the direction of shear. It follows that the proportion of the total stress which is affected by the viscosity of the substrate is greatest when the alignment is random and least when fully aligned. This is reflected in the temperature coefficient of the viscosity of the whole suspension, which should decrease as the shear rate increases. This can be seen in some measurements on an apple puree. For the purpose of expressing the temperature dependence an apparent activation energy has been calculated from the viscosity measurements at three temperatures, 20, 25 and 30 °C, and this has been plotted against shear rate in Fig. 29. This shows that as the shear rate increases by a factor of some 600 and the corresponding stress by a factor of about 10, the temperature dependence of viscosity of the puree decreased to about one-third. The curve appears to be approaching a lower value asymptotically at the higher shear rate end, as would be expected if the particles are nearing perfect alignment.

CHAPTER 9

A Yield Value and Its Significance

We may now turn our attention to a slightly different material. Chocolate is a little unusual in that it is a food that is important to the food scientist in both the solid and the fluid state. The state is dominated by the state of the fat in it. The natural fat, cocoa butter, is unusual among fats in that it melts quite sharply around 32 °C; most natural fats exhibit the phenomenon of a range of temperature, the so-called melting range, of several degrees over which the transition from predominantly solid properties to fluid takes place. Below its melting point, chocolate is eaten as a confection and the property of greatest interest is its eating quality. Although this may have rheological connotations, it is a textural property, normally assessed by means of organoleptic tests, and as such it does not lie within the scope of this monograph. Above 32 °C chocolate is fluid and it is in this state that it is handled during manufacture and where laboratory control may be exercised by means of rheological measurements.

Chocolate has tended to occupy a rather isolated position in the world of food rheology, almost as if the rheology of chocolate were a separate study. There is no logical reason for this: chocolate is just another fluid whose properties are determined by its structure. Indeed, it is not very different from the fruit purees; it is more of a slurry than a fluid, having a high content of solid matter in suspension. Most of the difference from purees is that, whereas their liquid phase is an aqueous solution whose viscosity is usually low, in chocolate the liquid phase is a fat only a few degrees above its melting point and has a considerably higher viscosity.

The single most important property in the use of chocolate is that it has a yield value. Most of the scientific effort has been devoted to a study of this yield value. Furthermore, the chocolate industry has come to an international understanding on the determination of the yield stress from the flow curve. It has been agreed that the flow curve shall be extrapolated to zero shear rate by the application of the Casson equation. This is an interesting choice. Casson derived his equation for use with printing inks, on the assumption that the suspended particles should form long extended aggregates, and by considering the rotation and the disruption of these under the influence of shear or flow he arrived at his well-known equation. There is no evidence that any aggregate of this kind may exist in chocolate. Nevertheless, to the casual observer, the flow of printing ink and chocolate bear some resemblance to each other and their characteristic flow curves are of generally the same shape. Nor is this the place to criticize the conclusions of experts in their field: the Casson equation serves the chocolate industry well. It provides it with clearly defined parameters upon which to base its technical developments and makes it easy for fellow workers to communicate. But the parameters of the Casson equation, however useful they may be and however accurately they may be determined, should be taken only for what they are: a convenient way of describing a presumptive flow curve.

It is pertinent at this point to consider the composition of chocolate. There are three principal ingredients. The detailed composition may vary according to the requirements of the market and of the processor, but about 30% of the volume is liquid fat and the remainder is solids in suspension. Of these solids about 70% is sugar and the rest cocoa solids derived by crushing the cocoa bean. There may be in addition small quantities of flavouring materials, such as milk solids, or of surface-active materials which are, in effect, plasticizers, such as lecithin. There may also be some absorbed water associated with the sugar or with the cocoa solids. Both the solid constituents are ground down during the course of processing so that they are generally amorphous. The particles may be as small as 10 μm in diameter, or even less, and occasionally as large as 100 μm. One consequence of this size distribution is that from the point of view of measurement the viscometer gap must be sufficiently large for the sample in the gap to be representative. This precludes the use of most cone and plate viscometers, since a single particle could easily bridge the gap completely, leading to quite spurious results. Also, if the idea of aggregates rotating within the mass is to have any chance of reality, the gap width must be considerably larger than their largest dimension. With a mean diameter of around 30 μm, it would not be unreasonable to propose a minimum separation of at least 1 mm between the plates in any viscometer used for chocolate.

With approximately 70% of the chocolate being solid, it is obvious that normal fluid motion under shear is not possible. Obviously, Casson's original postulate of extended aggregates rotating in a fluid medium cannot be applied to a system such as this and the agreement between the Casson equation and any practically determined flow curve must be regarded as purely fortuitous. Rather must the motion be considered to be that of a dense crowd of particles, with the liquid fat filling the void spaces and also providing a film which may lubricate the friction between moving particles. The particles, being amorphous and irregular, may be considered rough compared with the distance separating them, so that in the rest position before a shearing stress is applied there will be a random structure of particles in contact with one another at the tips of their asperities and this structure will have some rigidity in just the same manner as a heap of powder has rigidity. On the application of a stress, at first the static friction due to the contacts must be overcome, and once this has happened the fat can now act as a lubricant between the particles and flow ensues. As the motion builds up, some streaming may occur, causing the resistance to diminish, just as in the case of a thick cream, but it is much more likely that the decrease in viscosity arises from a gradual breaking-up of adventitious aggregates.

At this point it is worth while looking at an actual flow curve. Figure 30 shows some measurements made in a concentric cylinder viscometer on a molten milk chocolate. It is usually recommended that the Casson equation be applied only to measurements made at shear rates above about 1 s^{-1}. This is for no better reason than that experience has shown that at lower shear rates the equation does not fit the curve obtained. In the figure the stress and the shear rate have been plotted on a square root scale. This is sometimes known as the Casson plot. It can be seen that 12 points, covering nearly two decades of shear rate, lie on a good straight line. At higher shear rates the stresses begin to diverge from those given by this line and the chocolate flow tends to become more nearly Newtonian. If the curve is extrapolated in the other direction towards zero shear rate, there is an intercept on the stress axis, which is a measure of the yield value. In this particular example this yield stress may be determined as 38·6 Pa and the (Casson) viscosity as 2·83 Pa s; the 95% confidence limits of the yield stress are only ±0·2 Pa on either side of the extrapolated value. The equation is an excellent fit to the data and one might assert with reasonable confidence that the chocolate behaves as a fluid with a yield stress of 38·6 Pa, and this is indeed the value which would normally be quoted. However, if one were to carry out the experiment at lower rates of shear, as was done in this case, it becomes obvious that the chocolate flows at a much lower stress than the

38·6 Pa. In the figure, four experimental points where stresses were less than 38·6 Pa have been plotted as crosses. These can also be fitted by a straight line. This time the stress intercept (yield stress) is only 3·9 Pa and the (Casson) viscosity 132 Pa s. So that this chocolate sample shows two apparent yield stresses, differing by an order of magnitude, according to the measuring regime chosen. This point must be investigated further. Both yield stresses were determined by extrapolating to zero shear rate curves obtained in a viscometer in which the speed was varied and the

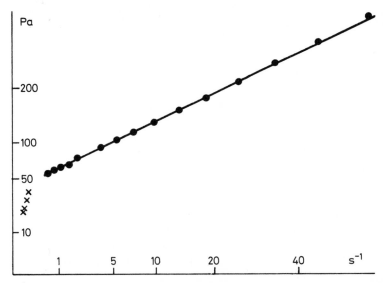

FIG. 30. Flow curve for a sample of molten chocolate (Casson plot) showing upper apparent yield value.

resulting stress measured. They were therefore only inferred values. If one wishes to obtain a direct measurement of a yield stress, the viscometer must be one in which the applied stress may be varied, increasing from zero, and the resulting flow measured. Another sample of chocolate, of different type and origin, has recently been studied in just such a visco-meter. The Casson plot for this experiment is shown in Fig. 31. In this particular experiment there was more detail in the range below the shear rate of 1 s^{-1} and it is evident that the upper part of the curve appears to extrapolate to a yield stress of about 3 Pa, whilst the lowest stress at which movement was detected was 1 Pa. Again, the two portions of the curve could be reasonably fitted by the Casson plot. The conclusion corroborates the earlier finding: chocolate has two apparent yield values.

This leads us to postulate that the rigid structure of chocolate at rest breaks down in two stages. On the application of only a small stress, cracks appear at the weakest points in the structure and large aggregates, themselves entraining most of the liquid fat, begin to slide over one another, lubricated only by thin films between them. The resistance to

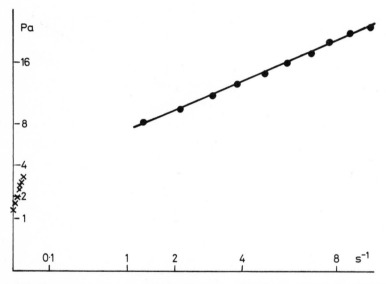

FIG. 31. Flow curve for a sample of molten chocolate (Casson plot) showing lower yield value.

sliding motion is high, so this is a region exhibiting high viscosity. However, the aggregates themselves can withstand only a limited shearing stress and as soon as this critical value is reached, they too begin to disintegrate. There are now many more lubricated surfaces so that the motion is altogether freer and this is a region of lowering viscosity as the aggregates break up. It is unfortunate that chocolate is densely packed and opaque. It would be an interesting experiment to observe the actual motion of the particles while the stress was being increased to substantiate this hypothesis.

We may bring one other piece of experimental evidence to bear on the problem of the structure. It was stated in the previous chapter that the existence of a yield value should give rise to a shear-rate-dependent temperature coefficient of viscosity. Another sample of the chocolate of the same origin as that used for Fig. 31 was examined over a range of temperatures between 40 and 65 °C. At each shear rate an apparent activation energy was calculated. Bearing in mind the comments on precision of such a determination in Chapter 6, the linearity of the Arrhenius plots for this sample was very good, except at the lowest shear rates where

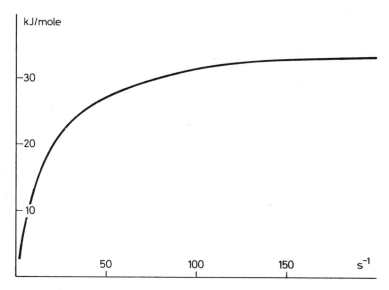

FIG. 32. Dependence of temperature coefficient of apparent viscosity on shear rate for a sample of molten chocolate.

the torque measured was small. These activation energies may be taken then as an accurate representation of the temperature variation of the viscosity. Figure 32 shows the variation of activation energies with shear rate. This is a very different curve from that for the apple puree (Fig. 29). Here it will be seen that the temperature dependence increases progressively as the shear rate increases. This is consistent with the idea that at low shear rates the main effect of the stress is to disrupt any structure, but as the stress increases, and with it the shear rate, so the viscous effect begins to predominate. As the particles are amorphous no reorientation can take place and the activation energy of the chocolate at high shear rates tends asymptotically to that of the liquid fat. From Fig. 32 this value appears to be about 35 kJ/mole, which is a reasonable value for a molten fat.

At this point we may return to the question of yield value. It is appropriate to consider what is the effect of the true yield stress not being what it is thought to be. For the purposes of illustrating this, let us take a practical example. Assume that in the process of coating a fondant it is flooded with chocolate at 40 °C, the temperature at which the curves described above were obtained, and that the excess is allowed to drain away for 10 s, during which time the temperature remained constant; at the end of this period it

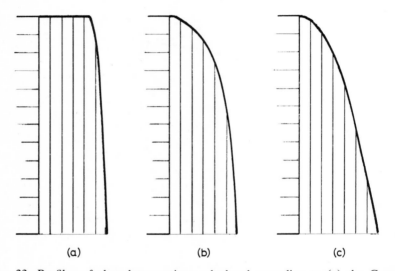

(a)   (b)   (c)

FIG. 33. Profiles of chocolate coatings calculated according to (a) the Casson model, (b) the true flow curve, (c) a Newtonian fluid.

is cooled rapidly so that the coating solidifies. The thickness of the coating adhering to the vertical surface may easily be calculated. Figure 33(a) is a cross-section of the coating on a 10 mm high surface which would be expected if the chocolate's properties were accurately described by the Casson equation calculated from the data for Fig. 29 in the conventional way, ignoring the behaviour at the lowest shear rates. This may be compared with Fig. 33(b) where all the actual experimental flow curve has been used to calculate the thickness of the coating. It will be seen that the Casson equation overestimated the total weight of chocolate adhering by some 2%. But it must also be said that an estimate of the weight of coating could have been made with almost the same precision if it had been assumed that the chocolate were a Newtonian fluid giving the same thickness at the middle level. The estimate of the total weight of the covering therefore appears to be relatively insensitive to the model chosen to represent the rheological behaviour of the chocolate. On the other hand, the thickness of the coating in the neighbourhood of the shoulder is determined by the behaviour at low shear rates, and here the discrepancy between the prediction from the Casson equation and the real-life situation is more marked. In practice the effect is less pronounced than in this simple example. For the purposes of the example it was assumed that only the vertical side of the fondant was covered with excess of chocolate at the beginning, no account being taken of any which had been resting on the upper horizontal surface. This acts as a reservoir and as it spreads under its own weight, the excess flows over the shoulder replenishing the supply to the upper edge of the vertical surface so that the vertical coating in the immediate vicinity of the shoulder is reinforced. We must come to the conclusion that, although the premises on which the Casson equation is founded are subject to question and they are undoubtedly not applicable to a material with a structure such as chocolate, calculations based on it give a reasonable estimate of the weight of the coating and hence of the average thickness and an acceptable estimate of the profile except near the upper edge, and even here the discrepancy becomes pronounced only when the drainage time is long. It will be fairly evident that the thickness of the coating is closely related to the (Casson) yield stress and that the vertical variation of thickness depends on the viscosity. The real yield stress, although it may have an important theoretical significance in understanding the structure of the chocolate, is of relatively little value as a predictor of the behaviour of the chocolate as a coating medium.

This situation may be contrasted with that discussed in the previous chapter. There, the reality of a yield stress, even though very small, was held to be an important feature of the rheological properties of a fruit juice. It is all a matter of time-scale. Whilst the properties of a fruit juice under very low stresses and at very low shear rates may be important for the manufacturer of a fruit juice, shear rates much below about 0.01 s^{-1} are irrelevant when chocolate is used as a couverture. It matters little whether the yield value is real or apparent: it is only important that flow shall be negligible within the few seconds that are taken by the operation.

It is not surprising that more effort has been put into studying the effect of composition and processing variables on the parameters of the Casson equation than into studying the fine details of the flow curve itself. From what has already been said, it will be deduced that the yield stress given by the Casson equation is a very close indication of the stress required to initiate the second structural breakdown in the chocolate. This is the breakdown that has been attributed to the disruption of the large aggregates into individual particles. If the hypothesis be sound, factors affecting the cohesion of those aggregates should affect the Casson yield stress. When the sizes of the particles are reduced, the number of points of contact between the individual particles in any aggregate must increase. Whether the resistance to disruption is due to the presence of any bonds between the particles or simply to frictional contacts, it would be expected that it would be higher the larger the number of particles. In fact this is exactly what happens. Grinding either the cocoa or the sugar particles increases the Casson yield stress of the chocolate. The sugar particles are on the whole larger than those of cocoa, but the size ranges overlap considerably. Because of this it is difficult to develop a quantitative theory for this effect. However, one may consider a very much simpler case.

Assume that the particles are uniform in size and arranged in layers, but that the bonds between them have a range of bond-strengths. If the number of particles per unit area is large, the bond-strength between adjacent layers will be proportional to the number of particles in either layer and hence inversely proportional to the square of the particle diameter. Now the condition of yield is that the bond-strength between any two adjacent layers is exceeded by the shear stress. The number of layers per unit length normal to the layers is also inversely proportional to the diameter of the particles, so that the probability of a rupture occurring per unit length normal to the plane of the layers is enhanced. If we now make the simplifying assumption that, to a first approximation, the shear stress associated with any probability of rupture is inversely proportional to the number of planes available for rupture and combine this with the strength of the between-plane bonds, we arrive at the simple conclusion that the yield stress should be inversely proportional to the diameter of the particles. Since the particles in chocolate are assumed to be spatially distributed in a random manner, the whole may be considered isotropic and it is quite permissible to replace the single uniform diameter with the mean without invalidating the argument. Some corroboration of these ideas is provided by measurements which were made on a chocolate in which the sugar was only coarsely ground, having a mean diameter of some 36 μm, whilst the cocoa fineness was varied between 10 and 16 μm diameter. The product of yield stress and particle mean diameter remained virtually constant over this range. When the sugar diameter was varied and the cocoa particles were very fine (about 11 μm diameter), an exactly similar result was obtained.

Once the structure has yielded and the chocolate begins to flow, the situation is less simple. It has already been pointed out that the solid content is very close to close packing. Since the particles are presumed to be undeformable, flow is possible only when they can rotate around one another and the smaller particles can fit into the voids between the larger ones. The ease with which this can be achieved will depend not only upon the mean size of the particles of each species but also on the particular size distributions of each and on the volume of each present in the whole. An excess of either very large particles or very small ones can upset the balance. Nevertheless, as might be expected from the fact that the stress required to initiate flow increases as the particles become finer, so does the apparent viscosity at the shear rates likely to be encountered in coating. At higher shear rates the effect of the unmatched size distributions shows itself. It is an interesting observation that the Casson viscosity, to which it has not been possible to ascribe a structural significance, increases with size of the cocoa particles and decreases with the size of the sugar, within the range of the experiment already quoted.

The addition of lecithin to the chocolate is interesting. Small quantities of lecithin added result in a reduction of the yield value and of the viscosity, but a minimum yield value is soon reached as the lecithin content increases, above which it rises again. It has been suggested that the minimum occurs when the lecithin forms a monomolecular coating on the sugar. However, the quantity which must be added to reach this minimum is far in excess of that necessary by at least an order of magnitude. If, in fact, the minimum of cohesion of the aggregates does coincide with the completion of covering the sugar particles by a monomolecular layer, what happens to the remainder of the lecithin? A suggestion is that it accumulates in the surface cavities, giving the sugar granules a smoother contour and thereby reducing the effect of asperities originally on the sugar surface. This would reduce both the yield stress and the viscosity.

CHAPTER 10

Plastic Fats

Another group of materials in which the phenomenon of yield value plays an important role is the plastic fats. In this group are included the domestic spreads, such as butter and margarine, lard and the vegetable shortenings. Unlike chocolate which has just been described, they do not show a sharp transition from the solid to the fluid state at a clearly defined temperature. Instead there is a wide temperature range, approaching 100 °C, within which this transition takes place, and it is within this region that they are normally used.

In terms of composition the shortenings are the simplest. These consist simply of a mixture of fats with, perhaps, small quantities of additives, whose function is to modify their surface-active properties with the aim of improving their performance in baking. These additives are unlikely to be present in sufficient quantity to affect the rheological behaviour substantially, though the experience with cream outlined in Chapter 8 cautions one not to be too dogmatic about this. The fats are glycerides of the fatty acids with chain lengths of up to 18 carbon atoms and which will crystallize in the form of long plate-like crystals. Additionally the shortening may be whipped to incorporate air or nitrogen, when the rheological properties will be modified by the existence of a foam. For the present, whipped shortenings will be disregarded.

Margarine and butter may be considered almost synonymous in rheological terms. Each consists of a fat mixture in which are dispersed water droplets whose diameters lie in the micron range. In most countries the maximum water content is legally restricted and since manufacturers usually aim to include as much water as may be legally allowed, this means that some 15% by volume of the butter or margarine is water. The water may contain dissolved salt which has been added for reasons of taste and also soluble constituents derived from milk. Again, these do not affect the rheological properties of the whole to any noticeable degree. There is also usually present a small quantity, which may be up to about 1% by volume, of solid matter, mainly proteins derived from the milk in the case of butter or from milk powder additive in the case of margarine. Again this does not substantially affect the rheological properties. Finally there is some surface-active agent, in butter derived from the milk, or added in the case of margarine. This is present only in sufficient quantity to provide a monomolecular layer on the surface of the water droplets, thereby stabilizing the emulsion.

First, we may consider what are the desirable characteristics of a marketable plastic spread. We must bear in mind that butter is a natural product, whose properties depend in the first instance on the cow, and which can be modified to only a limited extent by man's intervention. Margarine properties can be varied over a much wider range at the will of the manufacturer to meet the demands of his market. As a result some margarines which are produced for industrial use appear less like butter than others. For example, a margarine produced for the manufacture of flaky pastry may seem more waxy than a typical domestic margarine. This may be achieved by incorporating a higher proportion of the longer-chain glycerides. However, this is only a matter of degree. The margarine is still an emulsion of water phase in a mixture of fats and the rheological principles are the same. For the purposes of our example we will concentrate on butter and margarine for the domestic market, where the similarities are clearly seen.

In the first place the spread must be firm, so that it can be stored and handled with ease at ordinary ambient temperatures. If we assume as a minimum requirement that a block of butter in the form of a cube and weighing 50 kg is required to stand up without slumping, we calculate that the force on the lowest part of the block due to the weight of the butter above it is about 3·5 kPa. For the butter to remain firm under these conditions it must be able to withstand a normal force of 3·5 kPa without any permanent deformation, i.e. it must have a yield value in excess of this. On the other hand, if the butter is to be spread on a slice of bread, what is required is that a thin layer shall be left on the bread after it has been constrained to flow by the shearing action of the knife relative to the surface of the bread. Making plausible estimates of the speed at which the knife travels and the thickness of the layer, we arrive at the conclusion that shear rates of the order of $10^3\,\mathrm{s}^{-1}$ are involved in the spreading action. For the spreading to be effective it is necessary that the tangential stress which the bread experiences as a result of this shear rate shall not be so great as to damage the crumb structure. Combining the two requirements leads to the conclusion that the flow curve of an ideal spread should resemble that shown in Fig. 34. Readers of earlier literature on the spreadability of butter may find it a little unfamiliar to see the curve drawn in this manner. It has been drawn with the stress axis vertical only to be consistent with other flow curves in this book. The behaviour which this curve represents can be realized only if the structure which gives rise to the initial rigidity breaks down more or less catastrophically once the yield stress has been exceeded. The shape of the actual flow curve obtained experimentally with butter is shown in Fig. 35. Comparing this with Fig. 34, it is seen that apart from a rounding-off, the two are very much alike. The absence of a very clear point in Fig. 35 at which flow begins gives rise to doubts as to whether there is a real yield point or whether, in fact, the butter actually flows, albeit imperceptibly, however small the applied force. This will be discussed again later, but from the point of view of assessing the force required to spread the butter, the distinction is trivial. There is very clearly an effective yield point, indicated by the point A in Fig. 35, where the tangent to the almost prostrate part of the curve cuts the stress axis. The stress associated with spreading is somewhat in excess of, but closely related to, the value at this point. It will be seen that the spreading stress is relatively insensitive to differences in the actual shear rate involved, but is highly dependent upon the effective yield value. There are two important corollaries of this. Since the spreadability of a butter is known to be very dependent upon the temperature, it is the temperature variation of the yield stress, rather than the temperature variation of the viscous flow, which influences the spreadability. The other is that, if only a simple measurement is required to give an estimate of the spreadability, then one which responds to the yield stress is likely to be adequate.

Much of the effort which has been devoted over the years to the rheological studies of the plastic fats has indeed been directed towards establishing simple tests, with relatively inexpensive apparatus, which could be used as predictors of the quality required by the user. For example, various devices have been proposed for estimating the firmness or spreadability of butter or margarine. Whilst some of these have attempted to imitate the basic motion used in performing the subjective assessment, others have been purely empirical. Some of the devices achieved their objective and have gained limited acceptance. We may briefly consider four different devices. First let us take the cone penetrometer. In this a cone with its apex pointing downwards and initially

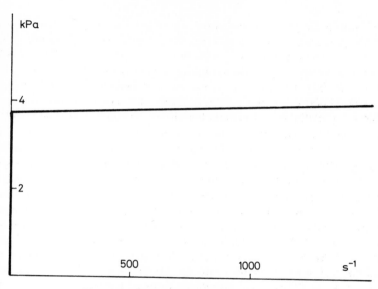

FIG. 34. Flow curve for an 'ideal' spread.

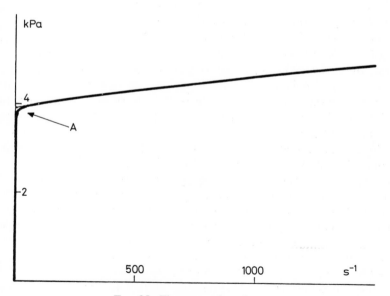

FIG. 35. Flow curve for a butter.

just making contact with the horizontal surface of the sample, is allowed to penetrate the sample under the action of its own, or added, weight. The stress at any instant normal to the surface of the sample is inversely proportional to the square of the depth of penetration: the measurement made may be either of the depth of penetration when the cone comes to rest, or the penetration after a fixed time, the time usually being fixed at a suitable value so that the movement has already become slow. This ensures that errors in timing and in measuring the penetration are kept reasonably small. If the measurement is made when the motion has ceased, then the yield value may be taken as inversely proportional to the square of the depth of penetration. If, on the other hand, some motion is still present, the stress corresponding to the penetration will be somewhat higher than the yield stress. However, referring to Fig. 35, it will be seen that the excess stress due to the slow movement is relatively unimportant and in such an unsophisticated test is probably no greater than any possible errors. Another penetrometer method measures directly the force required to drive a flat disk a fixed distance into the sample in a given time, starting with the disk on the surface. Obviously most of the stress is used up in overcoming the yield stress, and the method again measures a quantity somewhat in excess of that. Provided that the motion is slow, the excess is again unimportant for a simple test. In another type of test the force required to cut through a sample at a constant slow rate with a taut wire is measured. Once again most of this is used up in overcoming the yield stress whilst a small amount is used up in causing the sample to flow over the surface of the wire. The fourth type of measurement is of the force required to extrude a sample through an orifice. In principle this is very little different from the cutting wire test. An orifice is in effect a continuous knife edge, so that the only difference between cutting with a wire and extrusion through an orifice is that, whereas with the wire the sample flows past both sides of the cutting edge, with the extrusion the flow is confined to one side. In each of these four empirical tests the common controlling influence is the yield stress. It is possible to make plausible assumptions about the flow in each case and thence to calculate the position on a flow curve such as Fig. 35 to which the measurement refers. This is unlikely to be rewarding as the exact combination of yield stress and flow involved by the user in assessing the spreadability or firmness cannot be precisely defined and probably varies from user to user. Each type of test has its protagonists. There is no consensus of opinion as to which is to be preferred. Even at the present time discussions are still in progress with a view to adopting an agreed European test method. This is not the place to comment on the arguments for or against any of these tests, but only to point out that each is, within its limitations, fundamentally sound and is capable of making a useful contribution to the study of the fats.

The yield value makes a dividing line between two fields of study of the rheological properties of these materials. Much of the study of the properties in the region where the yield stress has been exceeded has been carried out, as indicated above, using one or more of the simple empirical tests. This is partly due to the difficulty in handling the materials in conventional viscometry and partly because the emphasis was on the technological problems and only quick tests were necessary to monitor these. It is one of the characteristics of all the materials in this group that any deformation of the sample is likely to damage the structure to the point where it will recover only very slowly, with a time-scale of weeks or months, if at all. And in like manner, any stresses set up in the sample during handling may only relax equally slowly. It follows that it is very difficult to place a sample in the sample space of any rheological instrument and hope to measure the properties of it in the undisturbed state. Some experimenters have used cone and plate viscometers and, by bringing the plates together very slowly, have sought to minimize the effect of any residual stresses. It is more satisfactory to prepare a sample in the form of a disk, cut carefully out of the whole, and to place this disk between parallel plates which are then brought carefully into position with just enough pressure normal to the surfaces to prevent the disk slipping when the viscometer is set in motion. This slipping may be further curbed if the surfaces of the viscometer plates are roughened. By this means the original structure in the material is disturbed least, though damage can never be entirely eliminated. If the viscometer is set in continuous motion the stress builds up rapidly until the yield value is reached and then a little more with the onset of flow, as would be expected with a flow curve such as Fig. 34. Thereafter, if rotation continues, the stress falls quite rapidly and ultimately reaches a value considerably lower than the yield stress. The extent to which it falls, which is an indication of the degree of structural breakdown, is highly dependent upon temperature. When the sample is butter at a temperature in the region of 10 °C the stress may fall to a value as low as one-tenth of the original yield stress. On cessation of shear the stress drops rapidly to zero, showing that there is little or no residual elasticity. If the experiment is now repeated immediately the same pattern of behaviour will be observed but the yield stress will be very much lower than on the first occasion and the breakdown correspondingly less. Although the material resumes its solid character immediately shearing ceases, recovery of the original firmness is very slow: indeed, it may never recover completely. Experiments have shown that as long as six months after the original structure has been destroyed the yield stress was still recovering at a very slow rate. It is an interesting, if not very practical point that, if a flow curve be drawn connecting the shear rate and the equilibrium shear stress, i.e. after breakdown of the structure, it is found that it is approximated by the Casson equation at shear rates up to about $100 \, s^{-1}$.

If, instead of direct rotation, the sample is subject to an oscillatory shear with an amplitude sufficiently large that the initial yield stress is exceeded, the same pattern of behaviour may be observed. The stress increases, more or less in phase with the strain, until the sample begins to flow. At this point there is a discontinuity and the viscous flow pattern takes over, the stress falling somewhat as the rate of straining increases, until the reverse motion takes over. Subsequent cycles repeat the pattern, with the stress amplitude decreasing with each cycle. Figure 36 shows a typical response for the first two cycles. Eventually there is no further breakdown and the response assumes a regular, almost square-wave, pattern as in Fig. 37.

When a small amplitude oscillation is applied so that the yield stress is never exceeded during the cycle, a very different response is obtained. The behaviour is much more like that of a polymer. The stress and strain are out of phase and, provided that the amplitude is small enough, the phase is more or less independent of the frequency. That is, the butter may be treated as a linear viscoelastic substance and a viscosity and a rigidity calculated. It turns out that the viscosity calculated from this type of measurement exceeds that which would be obtained in a continuous shear experiment at an equivalent shear rate. This contrasts with the behaviour of the aqueous suspensions such as cream, where it will be recalled that the steady shear viscosity is the higher.

Finally, the fats may be examined by a creep experiment. If a stress be applied to a free-standing sample, say in the shape of a cylinder or cube, there appears to be an instantaneous compression followed by a creep at a decreasing rate. On removal of the stress there is an instantaneous partial recovery, followed by a further slow but still incomplete recovery. It is not possible to describe this in any but general terms; the composition of the fats, the method of manufacture and the subsequent handling all exert an influence on the behaviour of any particular sample, but the overall pattern is the same for all. Figure 38 shows the typical pattern. This bears a superficial resemblance to that of a Burgers body, but the analogy is far from complete. Any parameters calculated from the compression part of the curve are different from those calculated from the recovery. It is

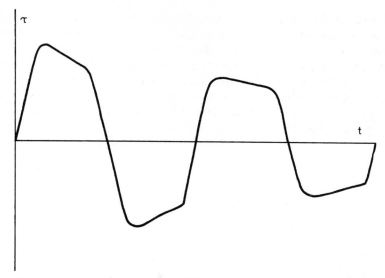

FIG. 36. Transient response of an oscillating viscometer with a sample of a plastic fat.

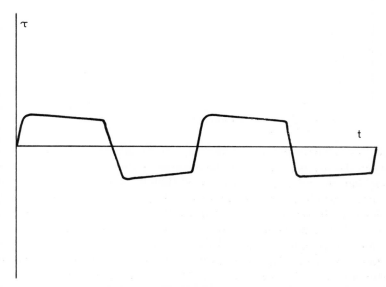

FIG. 37. Steady-state response of an oscillating viscometer with a sample of a plastic fat.

customary, then, to attempt to describe the creep compliance in terms of a larger number of viscoelastic elements, but this is not without its dangers. Once again we meet with the difficulty of time-scale. There may be an instantaneous compression, but all that can be observed is a compression at a rate controlled by the inertia of the apparatus. At the other end it is always observed that there is some residual compression which is greater the longer the sample is under stress. This final residual strain is sometimes regarded as due to viscous flow during the period of application of the

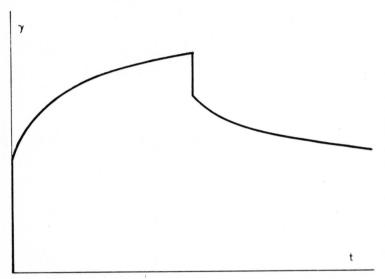

FIG. 38. Typical creep and recovery curve for a plastic fat.

stress and a viscosity calculated, but it is found that a linear relation between the residual strain and the duration of the stress is the exception rather than the rule, so that what is calculated cannot be a true material constant. It will be recalled that it has been shown that, after the structure has been modified or destroyed, it may still be recovering six months later, so that what appears to be observed as a residual compression in a laboratory experiment is not, in fact, an equilibrium value. Moreover, practical experience demonstrates that a large block will retain its shape indefinitely under its own weight, which is at variance with the idea that there could be any continuous flow. These experimental observations appear at first sight to be conflicting. It is important that any statement about the rheological behaviour of these materials which aims at completeness shall reconcile the apparent conflict.

It is a challenge to try to match the rheological observations with what is known of the structure. Returning to the composition, the principal component in every one of these materials is the fatty phase and it is the peculiar properties of that phase which largely determine the rheological behaviour. At the temperatures in which we are particularly interested, some of the glycerides are liquid and some solid. When they solidify by cooling they crystallize in the form of rhombic platelets, but they are prone to supercooling and when they form at or near the solidifying temperature they have a very slow rate of crystal growth and may grow initially with a needle-like shape. The fatty mass then consists of a suspension of these crystals in still liquid fat. Some measurements have been made on the crystals in butterfat: it has been shown that, on average, the axial ratio is about 4, with most of the crystals lying in the range between 3 and 8. As the crystals form in the absence of any external constraint, they may be expected to be randomly oriented. It is easy to see that only a relatively small proportion of the fat needs to be in the form of these platelets for some adventitious structure to develop within the material, giving it some rigidity. In butter only 2 or 3 degrees below the temperature at which the fat is a clear molten liquid there is already sufficient structure to provide some rigidity. One estimate has put the proportion of fat in the solid state that is necessary to enable a butter print to maintain its shape at a figure as low as only 3%. At lower temperatures more of the fat is solid and the structure becomes firmer. This, then, a random network of platelets enmeshing liquid fat, may be considered to be the basic structure.

In the course of processing, whether it be churning the butter or cooling the margarine or shortening and subsequently extruding it through nozzles, whether into prints or tubs, this basic structure is distorted and another, macroscopic, pattern imposed upon it. This pattern may easily be observed if a thin slice is illuminated from behind. Striations may be seen throughout the slice which show that the material is far from homogeneous. This often manifests itself during compression testing. Whereas a cylinder of homogeneous material, initially as (a) in Fig. 39, would deform uniformly to a new cylinder as at (b), in the fats there often develop cracks at the weakest point in the structure and this spreads along a surface between contiguous layers of the basic structure and slip planes develop, so that the sample may finish up as at (c).

We may now have the embryo of an explanation of the curved shape of the shoulder of the flow curve (Fig. 35). When the sample is first stressed, it behaves as any other rigid body—it deforms but does not flow. At a certain point the stress begins to exceed the strength of the weakest point in the macrostructure, a fault develops and some flow ensues. As the stress increases further, so the structure fails at more weak points and the overall flow rate increases. Eventually the stress is sufficient to break down the primary structure and the procumbent part of the curve is followed. The situation bears some similarity to that which obtains with chocolate, but with the very big difference that in chocolate the solid particles are amorphous and densely packed, in the fat they are crystalline platelets sparsely distributed. When the primary structure begins to collapse, the platelets may be expected to realign themselves parallel to the lines of flow. As their axial ratio is not very high and the liquid medium in which they are

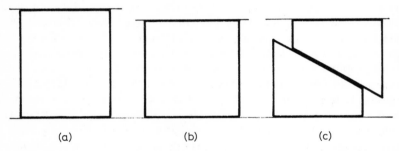

(a)   (b)   (c)

FIG. 39. Compression of a cylindrical sample of a plastic fat; (a) original shape, (b) ideally compressed, (c) fractured along a slip plane.

suspended is a fat only a little above its melting point, i.e. of fairly high viscosity, the time taken for reorientation to take place is appreciable and shows itself as the time for which the material must be sheared before the viscosity reaches its equilibrium minimum value. It is possible, though it has not been demonstrated, that in the process some of the crystals are fractured. It has also been suggested, and this is not improbable, that as a result of the work done in shearing and the inhomogeneous nature of the structure, local heating occurs which may cause melting of some of the crystals. If this be the case, when shearing ceases recrystallization should take place and be accompanied by the evolution of heat. Attempts have been made without success to observe this, but since the glycerides have such a propensity for supercooling and very slow crystallization, the rate of evolution of any heat may be expected to be very small indeed. After shearing ceases the crystals cannot resume their random distribution by

Brownian motion as they are much too large and the medium too viscous. The original structure cannot be reassembled; instead, damaged crystals may heal slowly, existing crystals may continue to grow and new bonds may form between nearly adjacent crystals.

We can now look at the deformation of the same structure when insufficient stress is applied to exceed the yield value. The primary structure to be considered is that of a lattice embedded in a viscous fluid. The lattice is strained to an extent limited by its rigidity and the amount of the applied stress and the motion is damped by the viscosity of the surrounding fluid. It is therefore a viscoelastic element. However, the lattice is not uniform, consisting as it does of a random array of crystals, so that it is not characterized by a single, unique, rigidity modulus. Instead there will be a range of viscoelastic elements which will have a spectrum of retardation times and rigidities centred around some mean value (the electrical counterpart of this is a resonator of low Q). Enveloping this primary structure is the secondary structure, which is another viscoelastic element of a similar nature, having its own set of relaxation times and rigidities. One would expect that the creep curve should reflect this structure. Some experimenters have analysed their creep curves and have found more than one viscoelastic element each with a characteristic retardation time. The number of elements which can be reliably identified is limited, of course, by the sensitivity of the experiment and the precision of the creep curve.

The most general expression for a viscoelastic creep curve is given by one Maxwell element in tandem with any number of Kelvin elements. (It will be recalled that the result of adding several Maxwell elements in tandem is to produce another single Maxwell element and it is not possible to analyse this into its original components from the overall response; Kelvin elements may, however, be added in tandem without loss of their identity.) At least two Kelvin elements are already suggested by reason of the two-tier structure. The presence of a Maxwell element in the analysis of the creep curve of a plastic fat is not so readily explained. There is nothing in the structure which has been put forward to suggest any mechanism which might give rise to unretarded elasticity. Furthermore, this elasticity has been seen to wane as the sample remains under stress. The other 'free' term, the Newtonian viscosity, which is given by the ultimate steady creep after all the retarded strains have been taken up, also deserves some examination. This viscosity has always been found to be high, of the order of 10^7 Pa s or more. Yet even this is at variance with the proposition that a rigid structure pervades the material, giving rise to a yield value, and with the observation that a block will stand for hours without appreciable slumping. If we apply Gent's approximate formula for the compression of a cylinder we may estimate that a block of fat weighing 25 kg and having a viscosity of 10^7 Pa s would begin to collapse under its own weight at a rate approaching 1 cm in the first minute. Clearly the viscosity must be several orders of magnitude greater before it can be postulated that any slumping over a period of hours is so small as to be negligible.

This is a good example of one of the problems which may face the food rheologist. Any discrepancy which may arise between the viscosities derived from the laboratory experiment and practical experience points to the need for great care in interpreting the data. The rheologist is at once at a disadvantage and at an advantage. The facts may be difficult to reconcile, yet at the same time there are often several experimental methods which may be applied for examining different aspects of the same problem. Again, it cannot be too often repeated that the time-scale of the measurements must be compatible with the time-scale of the phenomenon which it is wished to study. An extrapolation far beyond the time-scale of the laboratory experiment is, at best, an act of extreme faith. It may expose the experimenter to the risk of being dubbed a false prophet. Should an extrapolation lead to an untenable prediction, the rheologist would be well advised to reexamine the precision and accuracy of his data critically and if that survives the test, he should question the validity of his model. Whatever care may have been taken in making precise rheological measurements and in drawing conclusions from them, no interpretation may be regarded as satisfactory unless it predicts all the observable facts.

CHAPTER 11

A Case History: Structure Development in Cheese

The study of the rheological properties of cheese curd and the finished cheese is in itself almost an epitome of the history of the rheology of food products. It was probably the first food material to attract the attention of rheologists. Extensive experiments were carried out in the early days, using empirical and often ill-defined tests, to relate the development of the 'firmness' or cheese 'body' to variations in the technological process. The search still continues for simple measurements which can serve as controls, particularly with a view to automating the manufacture and dispensing with the human judgement which has traditionally been a characteristic of the cheesemaking process.

Cheese is also of particular interest because the development of structure takes place quite slowly and this can be followed alongside the accompanying changes in the rheological properties from the almost Newtonian fluid, milk, to the final, almost solid, hard cheese. There are many hundreds of varieties of cheese and within each of the major varieties there may be considerable local variations, ranging from the very soft cheeses such as Brie and Camembert to the hard ones such as the Italian Grana. The differences are largely a matter of degree, introduced by differences in the details of the processing method. Fundamentally, all develop in more or less the same way. For the present purposes only the general principles will be discussed.

The first stage in the cheesemaking process has received little attention from rheologists. Specific bacteria are added to the original milk to initiate the development of acidity and incidentally to assist later in the development of a characteristic flavour. The amount of acidity which develops is probably not sufficient to affect noticeably the viscosity of the milk. There may be a marginally increased tendency for flocculation of the casein particles and an increased tendency for the fat globules to aggregate, but neither of these is likely to be sufficient to be translated into significant changes in the rheological behaviour, though they may affect the changes which take place in subsequent stages of manufacture.

Next, enzyme is added and this attacks the casein. This reaction has been widely studied. It is a complex reaction and the chemistry of it is still not completely understood, but from our point of view the main effect is to cause the casein particles to join up. At the temperatures which are normally employed in cheesemaking—around 30–32 °C—this is a fairly slow process and there is what appears to be a period of induction before any change is observed. Very careful measurements on pure caseinate solution, using capillary viscometers, have shown that there is a slight decrease in viscosity during this time which is accounted for by a slight contraction of the effective volume of the casein particles. It has not been possible to detect this in whole milk, presumably because the contributions of all the other constituents to the viscosity remain constant and over-shadow this small change due to the casein. Suddenly, some minutes after the addition of the enzyme, the milk clots. This corresponds to the moment when the casein particles have joined up sufficiently for a structure to extend across the whole of the sample. Although this is the point at which rigidity is first observed, it must be emphasized that this is not a sudden onset at the beginning of the process. It is only the point at which the process of particle aggregation which had commenced earlier has pro-ceeded far enough to become manifest on the macroscopic scale.

At this point we may break off to consider the determination of this instant. If the viscosity of the enzyme-treated milk is monitored continu-ously, it will remain constant, within the limitation mentioned above, as long as no aggregation occurs. When the aggregation commences, the Brownian rotation of the aggregates will result in their having a larger swept-out volume than the singlets and the viscosity will commence to rise. At the moment rigidity appears, flow should cease, i.e. the viscosity becomes infinite. This is an ideal situation; in practice, the structure which develops in the early stages is a weak one and easily ruptured: it exhibits a yield stress which will increase as the structure grows. As long as the stress necessary to carry out the viscometry exceeds this, the clot will break down and an apparent viscosity will be measured. A curve such as Fig. 40 will be obtained, from which it is not easy to deduce the moment of onset of structural rigidity. On the other hand, if instead of the viscosity it is the rigidity which is monitored, as long as the milk remains fluid there is no response and the onset of rigidity is indicated by the presence of a response, the limitation on the precision being only the sensitivity of the detecting system. Two successful commercial instruments have been developed on these lines. The principle in each case is the same. A small alternating strain is applied to the sample at a low frequency and the resulting stress recorded. Initially a small stress almost a quarter of a cycle in advance of the strain is observed: that it is not exactly a quarter of a cycle in advance is due to the suspended particles giving the milk a small apparent rigidity as was described in Chapter 8. At the moment rigidity

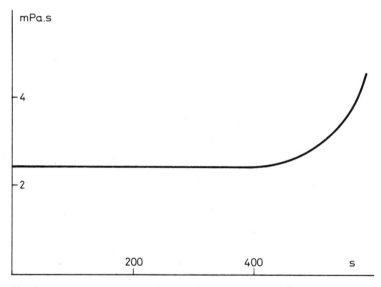

FIG. 40. Change of apparent viscosity during development of curd from a renneted milk.

develops, the stress begins to be pulled into phase with the strain and it also increases rapidly. The sensitivity of this method rests on the fact that the stresses involved in producing a small strain in even such a weak solid as a curd exceed those required to overcome the viscous resistance of a liquid such as milk by orders of magnitude. On the other hand, this difference in magnitude makes the instrument designer's problem difficult, should he wish to measure simultaneously both the viscous and the elastic effects.

An alternative approach for observing the onset of rigidity is to use the propagation of waves through the sample. Although this is somewhat different from conventional viscometry, it is still apposite to consider it here—the transmission of waves through any medium is controlled by the elastic and viscous properties of the medium. Of particular interest is the attenuation of any waves. A compression wave of a high frequency is rapidly attenuated in its passage through the liquid, but much less so when passing through a rigid solid. It follows that, by measuring the amplitude of a wave transmitted through milk as it clots, one can observe the development of any rigidity. A convenient method of carrying this out is to generate a series of small intermittent shock waves with a sufficient interval between them for the whole system, apparatus and sample, to have come to rest and recovered completely from the first before the generation of the second. In one practical application it was found that a delay of some 50 s between successive shocks was required. The method also suffers, of course, from the disadvantage that during the generation of the shock the yield stress in the very weak curd may be exceeded. However, the weaker the curd the greater the attenuation, so that there is some compensating effect between the distance the damaging shock will travel and the strength of the curd. The net result is that in the early stages the observed attenuation will be somewhat greater than it would have been had the yield stress not been exceeded in any part of the sample. As a result, any estimate of the actual value of the rigidity from the response of the receiving transducer will tend to be low in this region, but the determination of the time of actual onset of rigidity is only marginally affected.

Returning to the development of the structure, the casein particles do not form perfectly straight chains. We may recall that they are originally randomly distributed throughout the available space in a wide range of sizes and are in continuous lateral and rotary motion under the influence of thermal agitation, the Brownian movement. When two casein particles have joined up and are approached by a third, it is very unlikely that it will approach along the line of their common axis as at (a) in Fig. 41, but will approach from some other direction as at (b). Further aggregation will proceed similarly in three dimensions and the chain will eventually assume a 'knotted' appearance as at (c). This chain bears a faint resemblance to a helical spring and it will have a rigidity and a relaxation time. However, because of the semi-random nature of its formation we have again the 'low-Q' situation and the properties of the spring will have a distribution of values rather than uniquely determined ones.

There is another restraint on the growth of these chains. The casein already exists only in the space which is not occupied by the fat globules and the bacteria, so that the chains grow only in the interstitial space. If more than one free casein particle approaches the end of a chain, there is no reason why the possibility of each attaching itself should be excluded, provided that there are vacant contact sites available. Branching may therefore occur. This is naturally most likely where the casein concentration is highest, that is, in the voids between several fat globules. Ultimately there builds up a three-dimensional net-like structure with the fat globules and the bacteria held in the meshes. Thus we have a rigid structure whose rigidity is determined by the number of meshes. But since the intervening spaces are filled with the remainder of the milk, the fat globules floating in an aqueous medium, any elasticity in this lattice will be damped by the fluid present. And, as before, a range of sizes and shapes of the meshes gives rise to a spectrum of rigidities and relaxation times rather

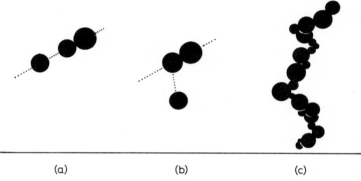

| (a) | (b) | (c) |

FIG. 41. Development of a casein network: (a) end-on approach of a single particle to a doublet, (b) approach from any other direction, (c) chain built up through collisions from directions at random.

than a unique value. The development of the structure up to this point is important as it has laid down the foundations of the structure of the final cheese.

The instruments which were described for determining the onset of rigidity can also be used to determine that rigidity as it develops. The figure obtained will naturally be only a single overall figure relating to the physical conditions of the measurement; it will not give a complete rheological description of the curd. Nevertheless, it does serve the cheesemaker since it will give him a measure of the amount of structure at any time and the rate at which it is developing. It is superior to some of the empirical tests which were formerly used because it does relate in a known way to developments which are actually taking place in the curd.

Moreover, the rigidity can be expressed in units which are universally understood. If a more nearly complete description of the properties of the curd is required at this stage, one must necessarily have recourse to experiments at the laboratory bench.

The curd in the early stages, indeed right up to the end of the setting stage in practical cheesemaking, is too soft to handle in the normal way and it will not even stand up under its own weight. A special technique must therefore be used to carry out any creep test. One device which has been used effectively is to carry out the enzyme reaction in a U-tube, so that the free surfaces are in the same horizontal plane as the curd forms. There is then no net stress between the two ends of the sample. A small pressure is then applied to one surface and the displacement of the other surface followed. The success of the experiment depends upon the curd adhering firmly to the side of the U-tube. If any slip were to occur at this surface, the whole sample would move in plug flow. Various suggestions have been made for minimizing the probability of slip. Roughening the surface of the tube is a popular one. But if any slip actually occurs, none of these is likely to be more than a palliative, reducing the overall effect rather than preventing it. Assuming that the adhesion is adequate, the displacement of the free surface will result in a parabolic profile as long as the response is linear, exactly analogous to the shear rate profile in the flow of a Newtonian liquid through a tube. From this displacement a modulus may be calculated, using the Poiseuille formula, and that modulus may be plotted against the elapsed time to give a creep curve. A relaxation curve may also be obtained by removing the pressure and following the recovery.

Creep curves obtained using this type of apparatus follow the by now familiar pattern. It is difficult to aver that there is an immediate initial (elastic) compliance, as the response of the apparatus is not sufficiently rapid, but the shape of the curve suggests that there may be one. If the creep curve is analysed, it can be shown that it approximates to that expected for a Burgers body. The existence of a viscoelastic (Kelvin) element is just what would be expected from the network structure which has been described. The elastic and viscous terms in tandem with it are less expected. It is always possible that the instantaneous elasticity is more apparent than real: if we bear in mind that the damping fluid is itself a suspension of fat globules in an aqueous medium, we may recall that in initiating the flow of such a suspension, before significant motion of the suspended globules takes place the suspension exhibits a transitory viscosity equal to that of the substrate. It is possible then to conjecture that what appears as an undamped compression is actually one damped only by that transitory viscosity and hence having a very short retardation time. Several possibilities may be envisaged which might explain the residual viscous term. If the network is truly continuous throughout the curd, it is difficult to see how it could flow continuously. It must be borne in mind that the sample is continuously changing as a result of the enzyme reaction, so that any measurements must be made within a comparatively short time. It is possible that the viscous term is really part of another viscoelastic element, but one whose retardation time is long compared with the time-scale of the measurement and therefore unobservable. Another possibility is that the mesh is not completely rigid and that some irrecoverable deformation may take place during the compression. Another suggestion is that the casein particles themselves are not rigid. It has been tacitly assumed that because the casein micelles are more or less round they may be treated as hard spheres and the resulting mesh as if it were composed of solid rods. But it is known that they are far from solid, but a porous array which has absorbed a considerable volume of the aqueous substrate within its volume. If some fluid were slowly expressed during the compression and through permanent deformation of the micelles were unable to return, this would appear as a viscous term in the creep curve. There is no evidence as to which, if any, of these possibilities may be a likely explanation. The experimental difficulties of observing possible small changes in the shape and the organization of the casein while the curd is undergoing deformation in the creep experiment are formidable. Other, circumstantial, evidence needs to be sought to resolve this problem.

After the curd has reached a certain degree of firmness, which traditionally was judged by the cheesemaker on purely subjective grounds, or may be decided as a prescribed rigidity measured with the aid of a suitable piece of rheological apparatus, the curd mass is cut into small pieces and perhaps heated further. During this time the curd shrinks and some of the aqueous phase escapes. It is a moot point whether the shrinkage expresses the fluid or whether it occurs through the progressive collapse of the mesh as the fluid drains away. As the fluid escapes, what was a mesh structure becomes transformed into one more like a honeycomb with continuous casein enveloping fat globules, either singly or in small clusters, with most of the aqueous phase being entrapped within the interstices of casein or in the now shallow layers between fat globules and the casein. This, then, is the basic structure of the final cheese. Rheologically we have a typically composite body in which the continuous medium is the viscoelastic hydrated protein matrix. The inclusions are mainly globular, and therefore essentially elastic fat, though again by reason of the temperature some of the fat is in the solid state, so that any elastic behaviour will be retarded, and these inclusions are lubricated by the presence of the aqueous phase. It is to be expected that this structure will give rise to a creep curve from which may be identified several retardation times and rigidities. As the cheese matures, the action initiated by the enzyme and the bacteria continues. In the hard cheeses the protein gradually becomes transformed into a more homogeneous but still porous mass, while the fat globules in clusters, having lost some of the protective shell of primary membrane and casein subunits by a combination of enzyme action and detrition, gradually fuse into amorphous lumps of plastic fat. The overall effect is an increase in rigidity.

So far, only the effect of the development of structure on the rheological properties observable at small strains has been considered. Whilst the creep test undeniably gives the greatest and most precise information about the structure, it is also exacting to carry out and may be demanding in patience, particularly when long time-scale phenomena are involved. It is therefore suited to the research laboratory rather than to industrial control. For routine purposes it is more convenient to use force–compression tests in which a constant rate of compression is applied to the sample and the resulting stress monitored. In practice this does not mean that the rate of straining (i.e. the shear rate) is constant. If the sample is originally cylindrical, as in Fig. 39(a), and isotropic, and is composed of material whose Poisson ratio is 0·5, it will deform on compression in such a manner that it remains cylindrical (Fig. 39(b)) and the volume remains constant. The cross-sectional area varies inversely as the height, so that the total force measured does not vary linearly with the stress, but varies inversely with the height of the cylinder. Furthermore, if the compression is finite, the total strain is not proportional to the compression Δh, but is now given by the integral

$$\epsilon = \int_{h_0}^{h} \frac{\mathrm{d}h}{h} = -\ln\left(1 - \frac{\Delta h}{h_0}\right) \tag{93}$$

Thus we see that, even for an ideal material the large strain response is not linear, though by a simple arithmetical manipulation it is possible to normalize the results. However, cheese is far from an ideal material. It may or may not be isotropic and the Poisson ratio is unlikely to be exactly 0·5, but for practical purposes it must be assumed that the sample is large enough at least to lessen the effects of any anisotropy and that any departure of the Poisson ratio from ideal is small enough to be unimportant. A more important consideration is the shape of the deformed sample. With hard cheese it has been shown that if the plates are roughened, because of the static friction between them and the sample, it deforms into a barrel shape, as was shown in Fig. 23(a). Lubricating the plates does not, as might be expected, overcome the problem, but instead results in overcompensation, so that the final shape of the sample is necked, as in Fig. 23(b). Because of these considerations the large strain force–compression curve cannot be so easily interpreted in terms of the

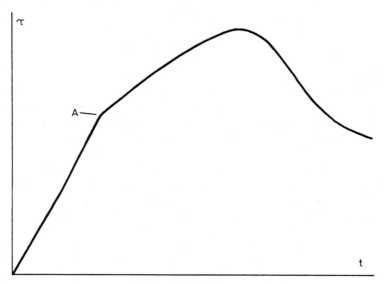

FIG. 42. Typical force–compression curve for a sample of cheese.

basic structure of the cheese. Nevertheless, it provides a useful practical guide.

If the compression is fairly rapid, as it usually is to enable a determination to be made within a reasonable time, the stress builds up more or less linearly at first. Eventually a point is reached where the slope changes and increases in stress follow at a reduced rate until the whole structure begins to collapse. Figure 42 shows the general shape of a compression curve. In practice, the experimental curve may be considerably less smooth than the ideal one drawn in the figure because of the lack of homogeneity of the cheese. Some attempts have been made to identify the principal parts of this curve with structural characteristics of the cheese. Only the initial rise in stress, which may or may not be completely recoverable if a relaxation experiment is carried out, can be directly related to the rheological properties. This part of the curve may be interpreted as giving some measure of the 'firmness' of the cheese. When the point of inflexion, denoted by A in Fig. 42, is reached, internal cracks begin to appear along the weakest planes in the structure and parts of the sample may begin to slide over their neighbours. As the strain continues to increase, these cracks develop and spread throughout the cheese, so that it becomes progressively less able to withstand the strain. Eventually the point is reached where the rate at which cracks develop and spread overtakes the rate at which applied strain increases and the peak value of stress is passed. The collapse of structure is not catastrophic even at this point. The peak value is not a measure of any ultimate strength, but exists only because of the balance between the two rate processes. The real yield point is at the point of inflexion A, where the stress is the minimum required to rupture the weakest cohesive bond within the sample. It may not be as clearly defined as in the figure, since there will be a distribution of these cohesive forces and the onset of breakdown may be almost insidious.

The usefulness of any parameters derived from the initial slope of the curve, the stress and strain at the point of inflexion or the peak values is limited by two important considerations. In the first place, they are not independent of the rate at which the strain is applied. It has already been indicated that cheese is a viscoelastic material, so that any stress which is being built up as a result of the continuous compression will also be relaxing at a rate dependent upon those viscoelastic properties. The experimental curve will always be a compromise between the two. It is true that, if an appropriate value for the relaxation rate can be determined, this can be used to correct the observations. But the relaxation time itself has a distribution function which may depend also upon the strain. For example, small shear experiments on mature Gouda cheese have shown that the relaxation times lie mainly in the range between 10^{-3} and 10 s, with a peak in the neighbourhood of $0\cdot1$ s, whilst large strain experiments have led to relaxation times of several thousand seconds. This relaxation of the stress during the course of the measurements is relatively unimportant if they are treated as purely empirical or comparative and are used simply as a control test.

A more serious objection is that cheese is such a heterogeneous product that the size of the sample may be too small to be properly representative of the whole cheese. This will be influenced by the character of the cheese itself; it is obviously more serious in some types of cheese than others and probably quite unimportant with processed cheese. In the case of a cheese such as Cheddar, where the inhomogeneities are on a large scale as a result of the method of manufacture, it is very doubtful whether anything less than a whole cheese is representative, and even that may not be representative of the batch within which it was produced. It is not to be expected then that measurements made on a small sample of a few cubic centimetres can give more than a rough guide to the shape of the response curve for the whole cheese.

CHAPTER 12

Some Large Molecules

The materials whose properties have been considered so far are all complete food products. The one thing that they all have in common is that they are all composite and that they are built up of structural elements which are themselves in turn built up from particles. In a way the structural properties and the behaviour of the products under the action of a stress may be regarded as a form of small-scale engineering, calling into play concepts similar to the strength of materials or even traffic control problems, as in the study of the movement of particles in suspensions. The observable rheological properties have been shown to be consequent upon the mutual relations between the constituent elements.

In addition to the complete foods, some of the ingredients themselves also have important and interesting rheological properties. One such group of materials is the thickening agents. These are usually grouped together as the hydrocolloids. They have little or no nutritive value, but are substances that are added, usually in quite small concentrations, to 'improve' the body of a natural product or maybe, in a manufactured product, to provide a substitute for the body of a natural food. A well-known example of this is the addition of thickeners to the so-called low-calorie soups to create the impression that there is a substantial content of food material, whereas much of it, which was probably mainly carbohydrate, has in fact been omitted. Another example is in the manufacture of artificial fruit juices and purees, where solutions of one or other of the hydrocolloids can be found which closely match the rheological behaviour of the natural products. At the other end of the scale there are the gelling agents, without which jams and many other confections could not be made.

There are only a relatively small number of these thickeners in everyday use. They are all singular molecular species, mainly polymers based on monomers of carbohydrate or sequences of amino acids. All show quite dramatic rheological effects in aqueous solution at quite low concentrations. Since they are single species, they have been amenable to studies by polymer chemists. Therefore, unlike the entire foods, whose formulations are at best based on grocery methods and which thereafter may encounter many vagaries of process, these thickeners have well-defined configurations and patterns of behaviour. It is not surprising that a number of schools have devoted their attention to studying these rheological properties and there exists a considerable body of well-documented information on them. Here, for the purpose of illustrating some of the points made in the earlier chapters, only a few selected examples will be given.

In considering the relation between the structure and the rheological behaviour of the aqueous solutions of these substances, we must bear in mind that the basic structural element is now the molecule. In the earlier sections the structural elements have been particles, to which could be assigned the characteristic properties of solids, namely, rigidity and permanence of shape. It would be wrong to apply the concept of solid or liquid behaviour to a single molecule. By definition, solids and liquids are condensed matter comprising many molecules and owe their bulk properties to the nature of the forces binding the molecules together into the whole. Individual molecules owe their configuration to the internal forces, acting on the constituent atoms or groups of atoms and also to the external forces acting on them. These external forces may be due to the presence of neighbouring molecules, or ions, or may result from the presence of a shear field around the molecule. Again, whilst in any particular environment a molecule will have a preferred configuration, at the molecular level the environment does not itself have the characteristics of a continuum. So the overall macrostructure must be considered as being built up as a result of local interactions.

A good example of the influence of its environment on a molecule's shape is to be seen in the lecithin molecule. This molecule contains a number of polar groups which have a strong affinity for water. In the absence of water, e.g. in a solution in a non-polar solvent such as dodecane, the lecithin molecule is essentially globular. There is no interaction between the lecithin and the solvent or between the neighbouring lecithin molecules and the solution is Newtonian up to high concentrations. In aqueous solution, because of the strong electrostatic attraction between the charged polar groups and the molecules of water, which has a high dipole moment, the lecithin molecules unfold and the solution has all the anomalies of non-Newtonian behaviour which have been described for concentrated solutions. With more than about 5% concentration of lecithin, the water and lecithin molecules form an ice-like liquid crystal lattice. This exhibits a yield stress, but below that stress behaves as a typical gel displaying a retarded elasticity.

The molecules of most thickening agents are much larger than those of lecithin. Xanthan is a polysaccharide which has an average molecular weight of several millions. In the dry state it has a helical structure with side-chains folded down along the helix, so that the molecule is more or less rod-like with a long dimension of several microns. However, the term 'rod' is not in fact quite accurate; it is not straight, but slightly curved, nor is it quite rigid, but possesses some degree of flexibility. By virtue of the fact that the configuration is relatively smooth, reactive groups are not exposed so that there is little or no electrostatic interaction with the solvent molecules. Furthermore, since the xanthan molecule is large compared with the surrounding water molecules when in aqueous solution, many water molecules surround each single xanthan molecule and the water can in this case be treated as a continuum. The net behaviour of an aqueous solution of xanthan is similar to that of a suspension of long rods. At low rates of shear, even with low concentrations, the rods, being randomly oriented due to Brownian motion, sweep out large hydrodynamic volumes and the viscosity is high. However, because of this high axial ratio, the rods quickly tend to orient themselves along the streamlines as the shear rate increases and the viscosity drops rapidly. Figure 43 shows a typical flow curve for a 0·25% solution. This shows very clearly the rapid decrease of the viscosity as the shear rate increases. At very low shear rates, that is those which were so low that the Brownian forces completely over-shadowed the stresses associated with the flow, and hence the molecules were able to retain their random orientation, the viscosity was 420 mPa s. At the highest shear rate at which a measurement was made it was only 2·5 mPa s and still decreasing with increasing shear rate.

The viscous flow of xanthan is almost entirely controlled by the hydro-dynamic effects and, when sufficiently concentrated, steric hindrance. If flow ceases the stress relaxes. The relaxation is quite slow and several hours may elapse before it finally approaches zero. Until recently it was thought that there was no interaction between the molecules and that relaxation of the stress would eventually be complete. However, more sensitive instruments have been able to detect a very small yield value in a xanthan solution at rest. For a 0·25% solution this is only about 80 μPa and earlier experimenters could be forgiven for overlooking this. In any case it is so small a stress as to be quite insignificant for any practical purposes. On the other hand, for even so small a yield stress to exist there must be a very weak structure in the xanthan solution at rest resulting from some interaction between the molecules. It is generally believed that, because of its smooth surface structure, the xanthan molecule has no available binding sites and so does not produce a gel at any concentration. Certainly no gel, in the accepted sense, has ever been observed, but perhaps the surface is not quite so universally smooth and the occasional binding site may be

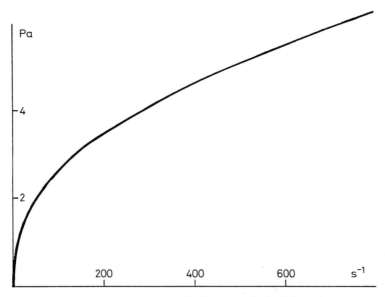

FIG. 43. Flow curve for a $0 \cdot 25\%$ aqueous solution of xanthan.

exposed to give rise to this extraordinarily weak gel with a yield stress of 80 μPa.

Also, arising from the fact that the major contribution to its flow properties lies in the dynamics and not in any chemical bonds, the solution is relatively insensitive to changes in the environment, such as pH or temperature. The absence of a significant yield value, but the very steep dependence of viscosity on shear rate, suggests that xanthan could be used as a temporary stabilizer only. One may imagine that it might be used to stabilize a soup for use at sea: it would be readily pourable, for in pouring shear rates of the order of 10–100 s^{-1} are involved, yet once in the soup bowl it would remain there in spite of roll in a heavy swell which has a period of several seconds and a shear rate well below 1 s^{-1}. On the other hand, this might be quite unsuitable for use in the dining-car of an express train where the frequency of the vibration is much higher!

It is worth commenting that the measurement of the viscosity of xanthan solutions presents some interesting problems. If we refer to Table 2 (p. 97) we can see that, for a material which is as pseudoplastic as a xanthan solution, when a concentric cylinder viscometer is used, the shear rate corresponding to the measured stress may be far from that given by the standard calibration. Furthermore, the correction for the end space will also be much greater than that when the viscometer is calibrated with a Newtonian fluid. It is true that, if the slope of the flow curve ($d \ln \tau / d \ln \dot{\gamma}$) is measured at each point, an approximate correction can be calculated, using either the method by which Table 2 was constructed or Krieger and Elrod's method. This is not entirely satisfactory, as it is just in the region where the correction is most sensitive to changes in the slope that that slope is small and therefore least easy to determine with any confidence. The most satisfactory solution is to use a cone and plate viscometer or, if a concentric cylinder arrangement must be used, then it should have a very narrow gap and be fitted with a guard ring.

As a contrast with the behaviour of xanthan, we may look at another polysaccharide, guar. This also has a high molecular weight, but it is a linear macromolecule with short side-chains which extend outwards from the backbone of the molecule. The guar molecule in aqueous solution is sensitive to temperature: not only does the temperature affect the viscosity, but once affected it may recover only slowly, or even not at all. This makes it difficult to reproduce measurements on the viscosity of guar solutions unless stringent control is maintained over the temperature history of the sample. At low temperatures the molecule has an extended configuration, but on heating this becomes less extended so that one would expect the behaviour of the solution to be less pseudoplastic after heating. In what we might term the 'pouring' range of shear rates, i.e. around 10–100 s^{-1}, this is exactly what is observed. However, the flow of a guar solution is more complex than this. Figure 44 gives a typical flow curve for a 1% aqueous solution at 25 °C. In order to bring out the points to be discussed more clearly, this figure has been drawn to show the variation of the viscosity, rather than the more conventional variation of stress, with shear rate, over some six decades. The most striking feature is that at both low and high shear rates the behaviour is almost pure Newtonian. This has tempted rheologists to try to fit equations of the form $\eta - \eta_\infty =$

$(\eta_0 - \eta_\infty) f(\dot{\gamma})$. One popular one is that due to Cross and may be written

$$\eta - \eta_\infty = (\eta_0 - \eta_\infty)[1 + (\lambda_c \dot{\gamma})^m]^{-1} \qquad (94)$$

where λ_c is a characteristic (relaxation) time and m is an even number. The theoretical justification for this equation is that it is dimensionally consistent and fulfils the requirements of sign. These are necessary conditions as has been stressed earlier: whether one accepts them as sufficient

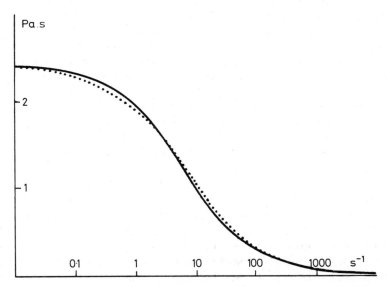

FIG. 44. Flow curve for a 1% aqueous solution of guar: ———, experimental curve; ⋯⋯⋯, best-fitting curve by the Cross equation.

depends on one's own philosophy. It is not an easy equation to fit to an experimental flow curve unless both η_0 and η_∞ are accessible experimentally. In the example given in Fig. 44 it is possible to make a reasonable estimate of η_0, but η_∞ cannot be better than a guess as the viscosity had not become constant, but was decreasing still at the highest shear rate of 10 000 s^{-1}. Fortunately the value of η given by eqn (94) is rather insensitive to the value of the infinite shear rate viscosity. As a first approximation the Einstein value for a suspension of long rods may be substituted without serious error. The value of λ_c, the characteristic time, is given by the reciprocal of the shear rate at which the viscosity is exactly the mean of the upper and lower limits, and this may be estimated from the curve. It appears to be in this case about 0·15 s, and the mean viscosity about 1·2 Pa s, whence it may be deduced that the exponent has a value of about 0·7. It may be remarked that this violates one of the original conditions and throws doubt upon the validity of the whole operation except as yet another exercise in empirical curve-fitting. However, ignoring this caveat for the time being, we may calculate a theoretical curve using these constants and this has been drawn on Fig. 44 as a dotted line. It is not a perfect fit to the experimental data, as it predicts a rather less steep dependence of viscosity on shear rate and an onset of the decrease at lower shear rates than was actually found. Nevertheless, the fit is sufficiently good to make a useful starting-point for discussion. Equation (94) was derived by Cross by making the assumption that linkages between the molecules were broken during shearing and that this could be considered as a rate process, with the rate proportional to a (fractional) power of the shear rate. The almost quantitative agreement suggests that the assumptions may not have been far wide of the mark.

We may now look for other evidence of a structure in the solution. Flow curves obtained at 25 and 35 °C are particularly interesting in this context. If the activation energy is calculated at each shear rate and these are plotted, the curve of Fig. 45 is obtained. At very low shear rates the viscosity increased with temperature, but as the shear rate increased the temperature coefficient diminished and eventually changed sign. It reached a maximum when the shear rate was around 3 s^{-1} and then fell slowly, appearing to approach a finite value asymptotically as the shear rate tended towards infinity. Whether the change of direction is abrupt, as drawn in Fig. 45, or whether the cusp is rounded off, is a matter of conjecture: it certainly occurred within a very limited shear rate range.

The positive temperature coefficient is reminiscent of the theory of rubber elasticity. That presupposes a structure with cross-linkages and a random distribution of lengths between linkages. By analogy we may propose that the guar solution at rest has its molecules randomly distributed and oriented, so that as shear commences some of them become entangled hydrodynamically. Since the distribution of molecules is random, the distances between neighbouring entanglements will also be randomly distributed. At low shear rates these entanglements give rise to the main resistance to the flow, and this, analogous to the rubber elasticity, has a positive temperature coefficient. As the shear rate increases, the stresses cause the entanglements to break up and the molecules tend to align themselves parallel to the direction of flow in the usual manner. The contribution of the streaming process to the viscosity of the solution has the familiar negative temperature coefficient, and the upper part of Fig. 45 is not all that different from the curve of Fig. 29.

If, after reaching high shear rates, the flow curves are generated in reverse, there appears to be but little hysteresis in the curve at any one temperature and that only at the lower shear rates. However, the derived curve of the activation energy shows a pronounced hysteresis effect once the shear rate has fallen below the point of discontinuity. The falling shear

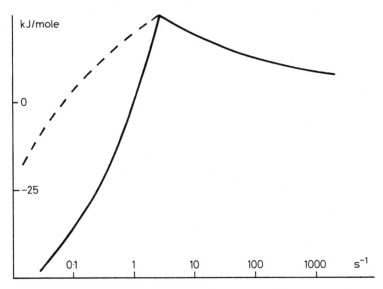

FIG. 45. Temperature dependence of apparent viscosity of an aqueous solution of guar: ——, increasing shear rate; ———, decreasing shear rate.

rate curve is shown on Fig. 45 as a broken line. Above about 3 s^{-1} the forward and reverse curves were collinear. This emphasizes the fact that two different mechanisms are involved. At the higher shear rates the simple rotation effect is readily reversible within a time well inside the time-scale of the measurement. At the lower shear rates the recovery of the entanglement (rubber-type) structure is slow and its characteristic time far exceeds the time-scale of the measurement. In the particular experiment quoted, equilibrium appeared to have been reached well inside 120 s. Evidently the recovery time of the structure is much longer than this. It is many orders of magnitude greater than the characteristic relaxation time of the Cross equation, which refers only to the rate of breakdown of any structure.

If the concentration of the guar in the solution is increased, the amount of entanglement, and with it the viscosity, increases up to a point at which the solution is no longer purely fluid and a yield stress is observed. The entanglements discussed above are envisaged to be the purely adventitious consequence of the spatial distribution and the configuration of the molecules and not to be held together by means of any other binding forces. When the concentration becomes high enough, neighbouring molecules may approach each other through Brownian movement sufficiently close for physico-chemical bonds to form. This is the beginning of a rigid structure. Assuming an equal strength for each of these bonds, the strength of the resulting structure will depend upon the number of these bonded contacts per unit volume, whence the strength may be expected to increase exponentially with the number of molecules available to form linkages in a unit volume. The rheological manifestation of this strength being the yield stress, this should increase exponentially with concentration, which is exactly what has been observed.

We may interrupt the discussion at this point to consider briefly the philosophical question which it poses. Is there really a specific concentration which is necessary for any rigidity? Or is it again just an expression of the threshold of observability? It is inconceivable that no bonds should form when the concentration is below a certain critical value. There should be a finite, even though small, probability of the molecules linking, however low the concentration, and a yield stress will be observed on a macroscopic sample only when that probability becomes great enough for an observable continuous structure to form throughout the sample. Measurements of yield stress on progressively thinner (microscopically thin) sections of a sample might throw some light on this, but these do not appear to have been carried out yet.

It has been remarked that the yield stress which can be measured depends on the method of measurement. If the stress on a guar gel is increased gradually, a point is reached at which flow is first observed. However, the value of this stress has been found to be dependent upon the rate of that increase. It has also been remarked that the yield stress determined by a static experiment was higher than that obtained by extrapolating the flow curve backwards towards zero shear rate. These observations are in keeping with the proposed structural model. Yield is not to be regarded as a catastrophic process on the macroscopic scale, though it must be catastrophic as far as individual linkages are concerned. The more rapidly the stress is applied, the more rapidly the individual ruptures will succeed one another and the more nearly sudden will be the manifest onset of flow. In the determination of the flow curve, either the sample is constrained to flow at a given shear rate, or a stress is applied until a constant rate of flow is reached. In either case, structural breakdown has occurred and this has reached an equilibrium extent for the particular shear rate. Extrapolation backwards of the flow curve must then refer to a partly disturbed sample and may not allow fully for the slow recovery rate of any entanglements or ruptured bonds. If the term 'yield stress' is to have any real meaning, it must refer uniquely to that minimum stress which will cause the onset of flow, however it may be applied and for however long. In practice, the experimenter may need to compromise over the length of time. In some cases it is fortunate that this is unimportant. For example, in the case of couverture chocolate, discussed in Chapter 10, the life-time of the operation for which the yield value is important is only a few seconds. Anything over 10 s is then a satisfactory equivalent to infinite time. When a measurement is being made, any stress which does not result in detectable shear within that space of time may be regarded as less than the practical yield value, even though prolonged application may prove that the 'true' yield value had been exceeded. On the other hand, if a thickening agent such as a hydrocolloid solution is to be used to inhibit sedimentation in a fruit juice, as was discussed in Chapter 8, the yield stress determined over a period of only a few seconds is not necessarily a good guide to the performance of the sample when a shelf life of days is envisaged.

When the concentration is high enough, most of the hydrocolloids form gels, though some may need the assistance of additional ions in the solution. These gels are characterized by an organized structure which is specific for each gel. However, from the point of view of the measurement of the rheological properties, with which we are primarily concerned, they all have much in common. At low concentrations, particularly, they are easily ruptured, which makes it difficult to handle them. It is usual, therefore, to form the gel *in situ* in the measuring apparatus. The apparatus, which is usually known as the Saunders and Ward apparatus, has already been encountered in the study of the formation of casein gels. It is equally useful for the hydrocolloids, especially the weaker ones. The gel may also be prepared in a viscometer, such as a concentric cylinder viscometer with the inner cylinder already in position. The formed gel can then be studied by either a creep or a relaxation experiment or by an oscillatory method at a succession of frequencies. The resulting curves are then usually analysed in terms of a combination of viscoelastic elements. This implicitly presupposes that these elements each have a strictly linear response and it is usually taken as sufficient justification for this that the overall response of the sample is found to be linear with respect to stress. The number of such elements which can be isolated may depend on the precision and accuracy with which the curve has been obtained. If one element predominates and makes by far the greatest contribution to the overall rheological behaviour, it may be difficult to identify with any certainty minor contributors.

The rationale for the analysis into viscoelastic elements must be sought in the structure of the gels. The gel structure itself is a lattice of which the individual molecules are the component parts. If the molecules were rigid and joined mechanically at their junctions, the structure would be that of a solid whose rigidity depended only upon the density of the junctions. The presence of fluid in the spaces between the molecules would damp any motion, so that a Kelvin body might be a reasonable model for the rheological behaviour of that structure. However, this is far too simple. The molecules are not rigid, though it has been seen that some are nearly so, and the junctions are not mechanical pivots.

When a gel forms, the structure may take on the organization that it does for one of several reasons. It will be recalled that an equilibrium situation is one in which the potential energy within the system is at a minimum. In a structureless fluid the equilibrium is labile: there is no preferred arrangement of the constituent molecules which could result in a lower potential energy than any other. In a hydrocolloid solution, when the concentration of the solute molecules is high enough for a gel to form, it may be that the net forces of electrostatic repulsion between parts of neighbouring molecules can be at a minimum only if the molecules take up a certain configuration. In this situation there is no linkage in the physical sense, only a field of force with a potential energy minimum. If the configuration is distorted, the potential energy rises in just the same way as if an elastic link had been stretched, though the relation between displacement and rise in energy may not necessarily be linear. In practice, for small displacements, it is near enough linear, so that the Kelvin model is again a reasonable approximation for the behaviour.

A more usual method of gel formation is by the formation of covalent bonds. The divalent cations are particularly effective in this respect as they can form bridges between two anionic groups on neighbouring molecules. The alginate gels are typical of this type of gelling. A gel is formed only when a sufficient addition of a calcium salt is made to a solution of the monovalent salt of alginic acid to create enough cross-links to form a complete structure.

A third method of gel formation is by hydrogen bonding, which occurs when free hydrogen ions in the water bind exposed groups, such as carboxyl groups, on neighbouring molecules and the aqueous solution then forms a gel without any further additions once the concentration is high enough, as in the case of the guar gel. The covalent and hydrogen bonds also have the characteristic property that stretching them results in an increase in potential energy and so these junctions possess some elastic qualities. The whole lattice, containing a large number of these junctions between molecules of a range of sizes and oriented in all directions, may therefore be expected to take on the properties of an isotropic viscoelastic material.

Most of the molecules which form gels are themselves large polymers which incorporate several different structural conformations. These include such well-known configurations as the helix, the random coil and closed rings. These in turn owe their particular shape to the balance of forces with covalent or hydrogen bonds or electrostatic forces again being the controlling mechanisms. These component parts of the molecules, too, will behave as viscoelastic elements and the stresses acting on them will be transmitted to them through the main lattice. The overall picture of a gel is then that of a complex mesh of viscoelastic elements. The rheological behaviour of the whole gel is the resultant of the rheological behaviour of the individual elements.

If the elements have sufficiently different characteristic times (retardation or relaxation), the creep or relaxation curve will show a number of inflexions and it is only a matter of analysing the shape of the curve to isolate each element and to make an estimate of its contribution to the whole. It is a property of each type of bond that it requires a specific amount of energy for its dissociation. This appears in the rheological behaviour as a temperature coefficient. If the creep or relaxation curve is obtained at more than one temperature, an activation energy may be calculated for the modulus of each distinct element. If the elements were acting in a free environment, this activation energy would be equal to the dissociation energy of the bond. But the environment is far from free; the forces within the bond are only part of a general force field and the movements of the molecules or their parts are hindered by the presence of neighbours, so the agreement is only approximate. Nevertheless it is sufficient to specify the type of bond involved.

From the foregoing, rather naïve view of the structure it might be thought that gels should recover completely, albeit somewhat slowly, after being strained. This is not necessarily the case. Some experimenters have commented that after fitting their models as accurately as the experimental data would allow, some excess viscous flow remained unaccounted. Others have raised the question whether the Kelvin or the Maxwell model should be used, although the Kelvin model appears to be the more apposite from the description of the nature of the bonds. Furthermore, it has been remarked that the creep curves and the relaxation curves do not always lead to the same analysis. For example, in some experiments on pectin gels it was found that the creep curve resembled that of a Burgers body, but when the relaxation experiment was carried out on the same sample and this was continued long enough for the stress to relax completely, a curve was obtained which could be better described by two Maxwell elements in parallel. It should not be entirely surprising that these apparent discrepancies occur. For possible explanations we may look both to the sample and to the theory.

The creep curve of a structured material is essentially a record of the progressive breakdown of that structure and the realignment of the constituent parts. Now it has already been shown that the rupture of a bond or the freeing of an entanglement may be a catastrophic event or at least one that takes place very rapidly, at the molecular level. Once the bond has been broken, the binding sites, and in the case of a covalent bond the binding ions, may move apart under the action of the shear or through diffusion. When a favourable conjunction of sites and ions reappears a new bond will form and the material will regain its complete lattice structure, though it will have undergone permanent strain. Although the motion will have appeared to be quantized on the molecular scale, on the macroscopic scale a succession of these discrete jumps would appear as a smooth flow. When shearing ceases and relaxation commences, any still ruptured bonds or entanglements may not reform, but similar ones may form to replace them. This formation is now a rate process depending on the probability of the coincidence of all the required conditions. As we have seen in the case of the viscosity of the guar solution, the time-scale of breakdown and recovery may be very different and this led to hysteresis in the flow curves. The same difference may lead to disparities between the creep and the relaxation curves.

It will be recalled from Chapter 1 that when viscoelastic elements are combined, some combinations give rise to rheological patterns of behaviour which are not specific for the combination. As an example of this, the combination of two Maxwell elements in parallel gives rise to an expression for the creep which may be written

$$\gamma = \frac{\tau t}{\eta_a + \eta_b} + \frac{(n_a\eta_b - n_b\eta_a)^2 \cdot \tau}{n_a n_b (n_a + n_b)(\eta_a + \eta_b)^2} \left\{ \frac{(n_a\eta_b^2 + n_b\eta_a^2)(n_a + n_b)}{(n_a\eta_b - n_b\eta_a)^2} \right.$$

$$\left. - \exp\left[-\frac{n_a n_b}{\eta_a \eta_b} \frac{(\eta_a + \eta_b)}{(n_a + n_b)} \cdot t \right] \right\} \tag{95}$$

This is of similar form to the expression for a Burgers body:

$$\gamma = \frac{\tau t}{\eta_M} + \frac{\tau}{n_K} \left[\left(1 + \frac{n_K}{n_M} \right) - \exp\left(-\frac{n_K}{\eta_K} \cdot t \right) \right] \tag{11}$$

Analysis of the curve alone will not enable the experimenter to decide which model is apposite. Some prior knowledge or other confirmation of the structure to be explained is necessary in order to enable the rheological measurements to be correctly interpreted.

In a similar way a dichotomy arises when the samples are investigated by means of an oscillatory experiment. The reader familiar with electrical theory will know that a measurement of the capacity of a condenser at a single frequency will not show whether the dielectric is lossy or whether the condenser comprises a lumped circuit of a capacitance in series, or in parallel, with a resistance. If measurements are made at more than one frequency, that lumped circuit model which gives parameters which remain invariant with frequency is unquestionably the acceptable one; but if the dielectric is lossy, its properties may vary with frequency and there is no absolute invariance. Exactly the same situation arises with the visco-elastic models. The frequency dependence of the measured properties may decide between a Kelvin and a Maxwell model and it is easy to convert the parameters of one to the parameters of the other using the relations:

$$n_K n_M = \omega^2 \eta_K \eta_M, \quad \frac{n_K}{n_M} + \frac{\eta_K}{\eta_M} = 1 \tag{96}$$

However, if these models are only approximate, phenomenological, descriptions, such as when the response is not strictly linear, then there is always some uncertainty in the conclusions which may be drawn.

CHAPTER 13

Conclusion

In the foregoing chapters it has been demonstrated that the outcome of any measurement of the rheological properties of a food material depends as much on the methodology of the measurement as it does on the properties of the sample. When the two have been disentangled, it can be shown that the rheological properties can be used as a guide to the structure of the sample material. Measurements made on selected examples of food materials have been examined in some detail to illustrate some of the problems of rheological measurement and also to show how both the behaviour of the sample during the measurement and the rheological parameters derived from it may be used to give some insight into the structure of the material. In some cases it has been shown that it is possible to deduce much about the sample from the shape of the flow curve. In others, where the rheologist is faced with unexpected results, or apparently paradoxical results from different measurements, it has been necessary to start with a hunch, or an inspired guess, and then build up a hypothesis, testing it along the way until a reasonably consistent picture of the behaviour patterns of the material is evolved. In order to achieve this, it may be helpful to invoke other studies. In particular, a microscopic or sub-microscopic examination of the structure itself, both at rest and in flow, can be very helpful in confirming what one may only be able to infer from the rheological measurement.

The list of food materials which have been discussed is admittedly by no means exhaustive and to some extent it has been quite arbitrary. For instance, no mention has been made of the foams (ice cream, whipped toppings, etc.), or any of the meat products, or of dough and bread. The changes which take place as a paste of flour and water is gradually transformed into a loaf of bread would have made just as interesting a case history of the development of structure and the changes in rheological properties which accompany it as the making of cheese. However, the underlying principle is the same. In each case the measurement technique which can be used must be matched to the properties of the sample. The main objective in the examples has been not to provide a mass of factual detail, which has already been published, but to show that there is a universality pervading the rheology of foodstuffs. There are only a small number of rheological techniques which can be applied and there are only a few basic structural types which can be used to explain all the patterns of behaviour which have been observed. The fascination and the challenge of food rheology lies in the ability to transfer ideas gained in the study of one type of material to another seemingly different one and to bring to bear all the available techniques to solve any one problem. In this way one may achieve a broader and more unified view of food rheology. Whereas earlier rheologists sought unity through a single mathematical expression, their outlook now appears unnecessarily narrow. What can and should be achieved is a unity of ideas.

Having shown that the rheological measurements, in which we are particularly interested, are a result of the interplay between the properties of the sample and the methodology of the measurement, we may consider how important this is. This brings us to the point of considering the purpose of the measurements. The food rheologist may be interested in at least three different areas of activity. If the main interest is basic research, then all the strictures and caveats which have gone before are apposite. There can be no compromise on precision and accuracy in the search for truth: the attainment of a flow curve, creep curve, or whatever other behaviour pattern is sought, as free as possible from error or the influence of external factors, should be the first objective. Only when the rheological para- meters have been disentangled from the methodology can serious discus- sion of those parameters begin. The accuracy which may be achieved and which will colour the reliability of any deductions made, will depend, as has already been discussed in Chapter 6, on a number of practical factors. If one may presume to put a figure on the accuracy which might be attained, it is suggested that an accuracy of $\pm 0 \cdot 1 \%$ of any measured parameter should be the aim. It may not be accomplished, indeed the heterogeneity of the sample itself may preclude it, but it should be within reach in favourable circumstances.

For routine purposes the requirements are rather different. Repeat- ability and reproducibility are more important than absolute accuracy. The precision to be aimed at may be dictated by the discrimination required between what is acceptable and what is not. It is likely that a measurement accurate within ±1% may be quite satisfactory. However, there is another important consideration. When measurements are to be made purely for the purposes of comparison, it may be unnecessary to eliminate the effect of the instrumental technique on the measurement. A simple comparison between measurements made with the same instrument may be adequate, provided that it is always understood that it is the instrumental readings and not the properties of the sample which are being compared. It is only when the results are obtained in different laboratories, perhaps using different instruments, that it is essential that the readings are corrected to allow for the effect of the instruments.

The control rheologist is well served by commercially available instruments. Those instruments of the force–compression type are generally designed to read out directly in terms of the instrument parameters of load and displacement. It is left to the user to apply any correction to convert them to stress and strain should absolute values be required. On the other hand, rotation instruments are more usually calibrated by the makers to indicate a putative stress and shear (or shear rate), the corrections being based on the assumption that the sample will be a Newtonian liquid. This presumably betrays their origin as purely viscometers. For routine purposes this is convenient, but if the user really wants to investigate the rheological properties of the sample, it will be necessary to recalibrate the instrument to convert the readings back to torque and rotation (or angular velocity).

Additionally, some more sophisticated instruments are coupled to microprocessors and minicomputers, which are programmed to carry out set test routines and present the results in graphical or printed form. These further relieve the experimenter of much tedious 'instrument minding' and ensure a high degree of repeatability in the performance of the tests. But it must be borne in mind that now, not only is the result dependent upon the interaction of the sample and the instrument, but the interaction of both of those with the programs of the microprocessor and the computer will also affect it. One must always be on guard against the risk that, in relieving the experimenter of the boredom, he has also been relieved of the rheology. Instead of the instrument being the tool of the rheologist, the rheologist has become the slave of the instrument. To take a fictitious example, suppose that a viscometer has been programmed to increase the rate of rotation progressively from zero and to compute the best-fitting power law from the apparent relation between stress and shear rate. Since the rate of rotation is never steady, an equilibrium condition is never established at any shear rate. The torque recorded at any instant does not refer to the steady state but is some transitory pre-equilibrium value. If the sample breaks down under prolonged shear the torque may be much higher than the equilibrium value, but if it exhibits an overshoot phenomenon as in Fig. 10, it could be either greater or less according to which part of the curve had been reached. From what has been said earlier it will be obvious that the higher the rate of rotation, the more nearly will the sample have reached equilibrium, but at the lower shear rates the stress may be far from its equilibrium value. At the same time, because of inertia in the moving parts of the instrument, the mechanical equilibrium will never be established. The extent of the shortfall will depend on the damping effect of the sample as well as on the instrumental inertia. The output from the instrument which is then fed into the computer will necessarily be a distortion of the true flow curve. The extent of this distortion will remain unknown unless one has some prior knowledge of the rheological behaviour of the sample. The computer will then evaluate the information fed into it as a consistency index and an exponent, whether or not it really does follow a power law. If all that is wanted is a comparison and some numbers to facilitate this, then the instrument has served a useful purpose, but it is not rheology. In general it may be said that, the more facilities that are incorporated to ease the task of routine measurement, the less useful is the instrument for the research worker. For the rheologist whose primary interest is in the rheology of the sample materials, perhaps the ideal arrangement would be for the rheometer to be accurately calibrated in terms of its own instrumental parameters, e.g. load and displacement, or torque and angular velocity, and then provided with the option of coupling it to a microprocessor and computer, each of which could be individually programmed at will according to the rheologist's own assessment of the problem.

A third use of the rheological measurements is to provide data for plant engineers to enable them to evaluate the performance of the plant as the food passes through it. The requirements are again somewhat different. If only the throughput is to be considered, the flow curve provides all the necessary information. In particular the equations developed for capillary viscometry can be applied directly to flow in pipes, provided that the Reynolds number is well below that at which turbulence sets in. The importance of assigning the correct model to the flow should now become evident. For example, in a pipeline of varying cross-section, a material possessing a true yield stress might cause a total blockage if at some point the net stress fell below the yield value, whereas if the yield value were only apparent and due to an enhancement of the viscosity at low shear rates, then there would still always be some flow through the pipe. Again, the velocity profiles, such as are shown in Fig. 14, are important in considering the heat transfer in a heat exchanger. A correct assessment of the residence time of the material in the system, and hence the proper appraisal of the performance of the system, depends upon selecting the correct model.

The properties which have been discussed in these pages all relate to stresses and strains in one direction. For some purposes this is admittedly inadequate. When any material is sheared in one direction there are also developed stresses in the other directions normal to the shear. These may be important to the engineer designing the plant, as they may have considerable bearing on the strength of the materials which must be used to ensure a safe design. The theory relating to these normal stresses has all been developed on the basis of treating the material as a continuum, although these stresses obviously arise from the relative motions of the constituent particles. The argument has thus come full circle. At the beginning the continuum theory was dismissed because it was inadequate and it became necessary to consider the interrelation of the constituent particles to explain all the varieties of rheological behaviour of heterogeneous food materials. Now it is necessary, in order to explain the phenomena in three dimensions, to treat the whole material as a continuum, having the linear stress–strain relationship already established by the particulate theory.

The measurement of normal stresses has proved to be much more difficult than making unidirectional measurements. Only a few such measurements have been made on food materials, not sufficient to make a comprehensive survey of them. There are a few well-known examples of the existence of normal forces. Perhaps the most often cited is the Weissenberg effect, whereby a sample of, say, heather honey will climb up the spindle of a rotation viscometer. Another example is encountered when one attempts to measure the properties of dough in a cone and plate or in a parallel plate viscometer. At low rates of rotation this is quite possible, but as the rate increases the sample begins to creep out of the sample space. At high rates it is thrown out quite dramatically.

Now, what of the future? Rheometers will undoubtedly increase in sophistication, though whether they will be any better for it may depend upon one's viewpoint. The quality of instrumental engineering is already high and it seems unlikely that there will be a demand for further improvements in that direction, though the use of modern lightweight materials may make a reduction in response times possible—and hence less dependence of the measurement on the instrument. Nevertheless, without any further developments in instrumentation, much useful rheology remains to be done.

There appears to be at the present day a growing awareness of the importance of the methodology of measurement. More international communication and cooperation within such communities as the European Economic Community or the International Unions of Pure and Applied Physics and of Pure and Applied Chemistry have drawn attention to some of the problems of getting agreement upon measured properties, and it is to be expected that the demand for more standardization will lead to a continued effort in this direction. Any progress in encouraging experimentalists to express their results in fundamental units, free from any 'instrumentation factor', is to be encouraged and it is hoped that readers of this monograph will be able to make their own contribution.

In the field of theoretical rheology, two current activities are particularly relevant. One is the exploration of the hydrodynamics of bodies in suspension, led by research teams in Cambridge, Montreal and California, which is gradually improving the understanding of the physics of unstructured suspensions and solutions, and very closely allied to this, the application of the methods of statistical mechanics, which can apply to both unstructured fluids and to those in which networks may build up. Progress in these specialized fields is necessarily slow. At present only relatively simple systems, certainly none with a complexity greater than that of polymer solutions, have been successfully studied by these methods; it is unlikely that they will make a great impact on food rheology in the near future as so many of the food materials are much more heterogeneous. Nevertheless, the serious rheologist should remain alert to these developments as they may help to further his insight into the peculiarities of his own product. Eventually it is hoped that they may lead to much more precise models, based on sound physical theory, which may replace the arbitrary ones upon which one must necessarily rely today.

Finally, in the realm of food science, there is still a considerable challenge to relate behaviour to the structure of the sample. Some of the examples given in the pages of this book are well documented, others are more conjectural. The rheologist can advise the food technologist most if he can predict precisely how the addition of any ingredient, or the change in any process, will alter the product. There is much research to be done before this degree of understanding is reached. More accurate measurements, such as are now possible, coupled with a clearer perception of what the measurements mean in terms of rheological behaviour, are a prerequisite if the challenge is to be successfully met.

Further Reading

In order to avoid breaking up the narrative, no references have been given in the text. Much of the material which has been presented in the foregoing pages has been culled from a large number of papers which have appeared in recent years in the principal rheological and food science journals. This has been supplemented here and there by a few hitherto unpublished results.

The reader who wishes for further information, particularly data on the properties of individual food products or groups of products, will find it most easily in those review articles which are published from time to time in the main journals. Those appearing in the *Journal of Texture Studies* are particularly recommended as they customarily are accompanied by a comprehensive list of references to the original sources. More discursive, yet none the less thorough treatment of their subject is to be found in books by Sherman (*Industrial Rheology*, Academic Press, London, 1970) and Muller (*Introduction to Food Rheology*, Heinemann, London, 1973) and in the section on rheology in Blanshard and Mitchell (*Polysaccharides in Foods*, Butterworth, London, 1979). For the reader who is interested in rheological theory, the monograph by Coleman, Markovitz and Noll (*Viscometric Flows of Non-Newtonian Fluids*, Springer, Berlin, 1965) discusses the subject from the point of continuum theory and also contains a very readable, though now slightly dated, chapter on experimental methods. This may be supplemented and brought more up to date by Walters (*Rheometry*, Chapman & Hall, London, 1975) which extends the subject matter to include viscoelastic materials generally and discusses some more recent instruments.

The reader may find on his library shelves other books which are equally enlightening, but if he has absorbed the distilled wisdom in just those few mentioned above, together with his choice from the references cited in them, he should be well equipped to keep abreast of current developments and to make his own particular contribution to food rheology.

The student of the history of theoretical rheology will find also that the monograph by Coleman, Markovitz and Noll is a valuable source book. It contains an extensive list of references covering the last three hundred years. Further references of historical interest are also to be found in Reiner's *Twelve Lectures on Theoretical Rheology* (North-Holland Publishing Company, Amsterdam, 1949). Surprisingly, there is little overlap between the two bibliographies. The theory outlined in these two books may then be brought up to date by papers published in the principal journals, particularly the *Journal of Rheology* and *Rheologica Acta*, together with the proceedings of the specialized conferences and symposia which the rheological societies hold from time to time.

Index